Endorsements

As one who has had his perspective of the spirit realm radically altered this book is quite revealing. I went through a major re-education of what actually is happening in the unseen realm as I received revelation concerning the "Courts of Heaven." The Lord, through many seer gifts has helped me to discern a clearer picture of the reality of this realm. Through Ana's explanation and experiences in this unseen sphere we can all be encouraged to *"look"* into this dimension. What we see can help us to adjust spiritual realities so things in the earth can be changed and reflect God's passion and will. Thank you Ana for helping us to *see behind the veil.*

ROBERT HENDERSON
President and CEO of
Robert Henderson Ministry and Global Reformers
Author of the bestselling books on the "Courts of Heaven"

Jesus is the one who said, "Blessed are the Pure in Heart." There was a promise that came with that declaration. They would "See God." Unfortunately, a quality that is not addressed enough in the prophetic circles is purity. But Jesus addressed it and so will I. This I know, the quality of purity will be greatly highlighted in the coming move of God. And the Holy Spirit is raising up a rare breed today who are highly gifted but walk the path of purity. Ana Werner is one of these NextGen leaders who walk in the grace of Psalm 24. Who may ascend the hill of the Lord, but he (she) who has clean hands and a pure heart. It is my honor to commend to you the lifestyle and the writings of one who is *Seeing Behind the Veil.*

JAMES W. GOLL
Founder of God Encounters Ministries
International Author, Recording Artist,
and Life Language Trainer

Ana Werner's book, *Seeing Behind the Veil*, is a thought-provoking book of supernatural encounters and adventures that demonstrate how intimately involved God is in her day-to-day life. She writes like she talks and her vulnerability is refreshingly honest and supernaturally natural. It will make you hungry for much more than you are presently experiencing!

This isn't a book to race through! You need time to let your heart move slowly through the pages, act on the questions she poses and absorb the revelations and mysteries of the heart of God she has experienced. What He has taught her are nuggets of gold that can be as life altering to you as they have been for her! Your earthly perspective can translate into a heavenly perspective as you spend more time with Him in the secret place.

LINDA VALEN
Ministry Director
Master Potter, Inc.
info@masterpotter.com
www.jillaustinlegacy.com

It's wonderful that Ana can enter Heaven and see beyond the veil. But what is better is that she has been commissioned by God to pull back the veil so you can step in!

It is a new season in God and in your life.

SID ROTH
Host, *It's Supernatural!*

Testimony is so powerful and impacting. Testimony imparts hope and faith and invites you to jump into the possibilities of that which you have heard and seen. Ana Werner's book, *Seeing Behind the Veil,* will create in you insatiable hunger for more of God and His invisible kingdom realm. Every page invites you to step into adventure and encounter with Him. Read this book and step into the journey.

DR. PATRICIA KING
Founder, Patricia King Ministries

Many Christians desire to encounter God but are not aware of the distractions that are hindering them from doing so. *Seeing Behind the Veil* by Ana Werner will not only make believers hungry for more intimacy with God; it will teach them how to position themselves for their own personal encounter as Ana takes her readers through her heavenly encounters with the Lord. Ana's transparency will bless readers and help them see that a perfect God is yearning to encounter imperfect people.

DR. CHARLES R. FOX, JR.
Senior Pastor, Christ Community Church of Bowie, MD
Co-author *William J. Seymour: Pioneer of the Azusa Street Revival*

What an amazing book; a transparent peek into the life experiences of a seer. I laughed. I had some "aha" moments. I learned more about the intricacies of a seer. I saw how simple seeing was (but not earthly), how reachable, and how God is beckoning us to come closer. The veil is thin! What a refreshing book Ana!

BARBARA J YODER
Lead Apostle, Shekinah Regional Apostolic Center
Breakthrough Apostolic Ministries Network

When I wrote my *Mornings With the Holy Spirit* devotional, it was an invitation to deeper intimacy with God through prophetic words He spoke to me during times of prayer, worship and everyday life. Now, Ana Werner is inviting believers to experience an encounter with God behind the veil. The real-life experiences on each and every page will encourage you daily to press into a place in God that is available to all Christians— but a place few dare to go. This young prophetic voice is issuing a clarion call to all believers who want to taste and see that Jesus is good and offering inspiration to continue seeking His face, His heart and His over-whelming presence. If you've been hungry for more, this book will show you what is possible for the one who walks by faith.

JENNIFER LECLAIRE
Founder, Awakening House of Prayer & Ignite Prophetic Network
Bestselling author of *Mornings with the Holy Spirit* and
The Making of a Prophet

In Ana's second book, her heavenly encounters with God (Father, Son, and Holy Spirit) and the angelic lead us into more and more under-standing of God and His ways. In spite of her frequent visits to Heaven, Ana is very real in discussing her personal struggles as a mother, wife, and minister, along with the lessons she is taught in the heavenly realm.

This is not a book to read from cover to cover in one sitting. Rather, the heavenly encounters she describes will lead the reader into pausing to reflect on their own relationship with the Lord and learning, along with Ana, how to walk out this Christian life. We heartily recommend this book. We know and love Ana; she is real, unpretentious, honest and full of love for the Lord, her family, and her friends.

DORIS and LEE HARMS
Directors, Heartland Healing Rooms

Anybody who encounters Ana Werner is immediately drawn in by her honesty, passion, and absolute devotion to Jesus. She is one of the most promising prophetic voices I've encountered in the past few years. I'm certain that her latest book, *Seeing Behind the Veil*, will bring readers great insight and unlock a whole new level of encounters with the Holy Spirit.

SHAUN TABATT
Host of *The Shaun Tabatt Show*

As I was reading the pages of this book I found the Spirit of revelation coming upon me. I felt inspired and experienced an activation of the revelatory realm to increase my intimacy with God opening up to me! I believe as you read this book, you will have the same experience! You will be able to come to know Jesus in a way you did not know Him before!

PASTOR TONY KEMP
Tony Kemp Ministries, Quincy, IL

Ana Werner's lifestyle comes from a desire to hear and please God. *Seeing Behind the Veil* beautifully portrays her encounters in the heavenly realm. I have great confidence in Ana as God has given her a proven ministry. She has helped me understand dreams in my own life. I'm confident *Seeing Behind the Veil* will be a blessing in your life.

DR. MARILYN HICKEY
President and Founder, Marilyn Hickey Ministries

What a glorious deep well of revelation Ana Werner's book *Seeing Behind the Veil* is! This book is dripping with impartation for you to encounter Him like never before, to experience His heart and heavenly realities that He has stored for you. This book will ignite hunger within you to know Him more and engage with Him in heavenly places! His Spirit will refresh you through the encounters Ana so freely and beautifully shares to take you to a place of deeper intimacy with Jesus! What a gift!

LANA VAWSER
International Prophetic Voice, Speaker and Author
www.lanavawser.com

Ever since I've known Ana Werner, I have noticed a measurable increase in my ability to prophetically "see" in the spirit. Thus, I believe she carries a genuine impartation to help others operate and function in the prophetic realms that she does. Ana is a friend and someone I have a high level of respect for. When I personally receive prophetic words, I present them to her for review, insight and feedback because of her intuneness with the heart of God and love for the Word of God. And yet, the most unique thing about Ana is not simply her ability to see into the spirit realm, have encounters in Heaven, and operate in the prophetic—all powerful gifts, yes. But she carries an imparting grace to help every believer enter into and experience new, supernatural dimensions of encounter with the Holy Spirit. Reading *Seeing Behind the Veil* is like sitting with Ana, listening to her life-changing stories of supernatural encounters with God and providing practical teaching on how you too can enter into new dimensions of Holy Spirit encounter.

With *Seeing Behind the Veil*, Ana delivers a real treasure to every spiritually thirsty believer. Whether you presently are hungry to know and encounter God in a deeper way, or maybe you want to be hungry, either way, this book provides 100 powerful invitations into new dimensions of intimacy with God. Remember, Jesus' blood tore the veil of separation between humanity and God. This book will help you access the supernatural dimensions of the Spirit that Jesus made available to every believer!

LARRY SPARKS, MDIV.
Publisher, Destiny Image
Author of *Breakthrough Faith, The Fire That Never Sleeps*
(with Michael Brown and John Kilpatrick)
and co-author of *Arise* with Patricia King
Lawrencesparks.com

OTHER DESTINY IMAGE BOOKS BY ANA WERNER

The Seer's Path

seeing
behind the
veil

100 Invitations to Intimate Encounters
with the Holy Spirit

Ana Werner

DESTINY IMAGE® PUBLISHERS, INC.

P.O. Box 310, Shippensburg, PA 17257-0310

"Promoting Inspired Lives."

This book and all other Destiny Image and Destiny Image Fiction books are available at Christian bookstores and distributors worldwide.

Cover design by Eileen Rockwell
Interior design by Terry Clifton

For more information on foreign distributors, call 717-532-3040.
Or reach us on the Internet: www.destinyimage.com

ISBN 13 TP: 978-0-7684-4283-0
ISBN 13 EBook: 978-0-7684-4284-7
LP: 978-0-7684-4810-8
HC : 978-0-7684-4285-4

For Worldwide Distribution, Printed in the U.S.A.
1 2 3 4 5 6 / 21 20 19 18

Dedication

I DEDICATE THIS BOOK TO MY CHILDREN. MY GREATEST DESIRE FOR you is that you may fall passionately in love with Jesus, come to know His love with your whole being, and run hard after Him with all your heart. May my ceiling be your floor and may you launch further into seeing in the supernatural with God than I ever have. May Holy Spirit become your Best Friend and may you enter into a divine partnership with Him. Always remember, my loves, you were created to shine! Be lights unto this world.

Acknowledgments

THE PRODUCTION OF THIS BOOK WAS ONCE A DREAM OF MINE LONG ago. As I sat in my little office, next to my fireplace on a wintery day, Holy Spirit breathed the idea of a couple of books into me. Without Holy Spirit's help, I could have never written this book and also walk with the Lord the way I do. So, to my Best Friend, Holy Spirit, I am forever grateful.

Sam, my loving husband, you are my treasure. The way you stand behind me, support me, and speak confidence into the wild and crazy dreams I have with God—you are such a steady rock for me. I am so thankful for your support through the countless hours that went into the writing of this book.

Thank you to my parents for being an example of Christ, covering me in your prayers, supporting me and my family in all the ways you do, and always letting me be who God has called me to be. You are my biggest cheerleaders!

Thank you to all my family and close friends that pray for us. My faithful intercessors, you carry me and the ministry!

My armor-bearer and assistant, Melissa Shirley, thank you for all the ways you carry me. Your prophetic anointing and prayers are precise and on target! You are one anointed woman of God, and I am so grateful to have you in my life.

Larry Sparks, my publisher and friend. Thank you for your walk with Holy Spirit, obedience to the voice of the Lord, and belief in authors who cross your way. I am so grateful for Destiny Image's hard work and dedication to stick it out with me throughout this process.

I also must acknowledge my wonderful kiddos who were the inspiration behind the writing of this book. You guys bring me so much joy every day, and I love being your momma with all my heart!

Contents

Introduction

SUDDENLY I FOUND MYSELF IN AN ENCOUNTER LIKE NO OTHER. There before my eyes was a shimmering, translucent veil. I could see shadows behind it and could overhear voices talking. Quickly, I realized I was hearing God, the Son, and Holy Spirit's conversations. Although Three-in-One, I heard them each responding to each other.

One voice that I learned to be Holy Spirit's, said, "I am so excited about the fire that's about to fall on China and Korea. Another outpouring. Another outpouring!"

"Yes. Yes!" I heard the Father say. "I love My Bride there so much. So many more souls to win, but their hunger and dedication is so beautiful."

Then Jesus' voice jumped in, "There's an outbreak of My Spirit in the Middle East."

"I see them. Arise, My warrior Bride. May your strength be renewed," God responded.

"Let's send help quickly," Holy Spirit excitedly piped in.

"America, America, come back to the Word. May your hunger for My Word increase. You are starving," God yearningly spoke.

I just listened. I held my breath in fear that if I was heard, they would stop talking. The heaviness of each phrase weighed on me like bricks. I was frozen, pondering them all.

Just then, the veil was pulled back, and Jesus popped His head through and smiled at me.

"My Lord," I gasped.

"Ana, come closer. Don't you know. It's your place as a seer to help pull back the veil so others can step into deep encounters. Come a little closer, My Bride. The veil is thin." And then He paused. "I'm coming, Ana. I'm coming for My Bride!"

And then, just like that, I found myself out of the encounter, lying on the floor of my office. I flipped open my Bible, and Revelation 4 popped out at me.

> John writes, "I saw a heavenly portal open before me, and the same trumpet-voice I heard speaking with me at the beginning broke the silence and said, "Ascend into this realm! I want to reveal to you what must happen after this" (Revelation 4:1 The Passion Translation).

I am convinced, after this encounter, that the veil between us and Heaven is growing thinner. As we approach the last days before Jesus returns for His beautiful Bride, He is making Heaven and the supernatural more accessible. It's for everyone, not just the elite.

So would you journey with me? Every word I have written in this book reflects my personal encounters from Heaven, Jesus, the Father, Holy Spirit, angels, and the supernatural. I have journals filled, but I chose the encounters that the Lord highlighted to me as the meat. I wrote this book thinking, *What can I pass on to my children from everything I have experienced.*

Each are invitations, really. As your eyes fall on the pages of this book, I pray the Lord leads you into your own deep encounters with His heart. He's coming for you! "Come a little closer, My Bride."

1

Tucked In

Just as I was putting my daughter down for her nap (I so look forward to that daily nap!), she did the oddest thing. She was 13 months of age, yet suddenly she did what she did as a newborn. She turned her head and body to the side, tucked herself in the bend of my arms, and rested her head on my chest and drifted off to sleep.

Instantly, God gave me a vision. I saw a soft but ginormous bird. There I was, running to the bird and tucking myself under the covering of its soft wings where I felt safe, warm, and as if, *This is where I need to be!*

Then I was back from the vision, and my daughter was drooling away on my chest, gently cooing. I put her in her crib and flipped open my Bible.

> *He who dwells in the shelter of the Most High will abide in the shadow of the Almighty* (Psalm 91:1 NIV).

OK, God, I thought, I get it!

As a mother of a toddler, lately I had felt my life spinning. Trying to keep up with my own personal deadlines, never-ending lists, Thanksgiving recipes to look up, Christmas vacation to plan, a husband who had now started working from home, and a toddler demanding *all* of my attention, life felt like a victory if I could move from one hectic day to the next without losing my patience and kindness.

And then God shows me this vision. Making it all the more real by giving me a living example of my drooling baby, all snug in my arms. He caught my attention!

In all the busyness of this season, I had forgotten what it felt like to dwell with Him. To just sit and rest for a second in His presence—and from that place, live! *It's time for things to change,* I thought. *He has to come first, and His presence has to be the most important part of my day.*

Breathe in His presence. Breathe in His peace, grace, forgiveness, and fullness of joy. Did you do it? Literally, shut your eyes, and try to see yourself with Him. Maybe it helps to envision yourself being tucked into the sweet safety of a warm bird (like Jesus showed me), or resting your hand in His. There is safety and peace in His presence! Breathe Him in, and exhale the stress of the day. Exhale the things that demand your attention, and just get full of Him first.

2

A Day of Complaint

*God, I feel like all my friends are able to pursue
ministry and all their dreams. I used to be that
way. I would run after any opportunity to minister
and serve You. We traveled all around the world
preaching the Gospel. Now, I'm stuck in my living
room! I'm stuck at home! God, don't get me wrong.
I love this season of my life, but sometimes it's just
so frustrating when I feel like others are passing
me by as they run off and pursue their careers.*

THIS CONVERSATION WAS NOT MY BEST MOMENT WITH GOD. I'M NOT
proud of it, but there it was. I woke up with nothing but complaints
pouring out of my heart to the Lord. I used to believe that complaining was sinful. In all honesty, as I ministered to people going through
a rough season in their lives, at times I think I lacked compassion.

Then I became a mom. In my place of weak moments, I learned
to embrace the other side of the cross. Suddenly, I became distinctly
aware, that although not good to dwell in it, it was OK to lament a
little to Jesus. God is big enough to handle my small complaints, to

6

handle my tears. The perfectionist in me was radically brought to my attention—my own need to live my spiritual life with God with a perfectionist mentality—like I had it all together.

That's what I love about David. Throughout the Book of Psalms, we see David's inner dialog with God. A man after God's own heart isn't afraid to be real with God, even in his weak times, and cry out to Him. He laments and then praises God. This is a great model for us! God's not afraid of our raw moments, so why are we afraid to be raw with Him sometimes?

After I had my raw and intimate moment with God, He took me into a vision. The Lion of Judah approached me. At first I felt a little bit of shame. *Why oh why did I just spend time complaining to Him,* I thought to myself. He approached me and rubbed up against me. I immediately melted into that giant Lion's soft fur. His embrace felt reassuring. It's all I needed.

Then the Lord spoke life into me. I heard, "Ana, you are doing just what I called you to do for this season. You are an excellent mother, wife, and writer. That's all I have for you in this season. That's enough for you, and you are doing it with excellence!"

> *For in the day of trouble He will conceal me in His tabernacle; in the secret place of His tent He will hide me; He will lift me up on a rock* (Psalm 27:5).

Not out of the perfection or performance does He love. He does life with you and me. Are you doing life with Him? Don't let your own insecurities or shortcomings place distance between you and the Father. He's right here, in the midst of it all, wanting to do life with you.

3

The Day I Lost
My Phone

OH, WHAT WOULD WE DO WITHOUT OUR PHONES AND TECHNOLOGY? I mean, really! I feel sometimes as a mom, that my phone is my life line; my connection to the outside world.

I asked my husband one night when we were sitting on the couch, "Do you remember when we had phones in India and Nepal that hardly ever worked? Do you remember what that was like, having no phone?" Funny that after being back for two years after having lived overseas as missionaries for two years, how quickly we've slipped back into the culture here.

So, one day I lost my phone and it was amazing! The following are the differences in my day that I noticed:

I was present. I took my daughter to the park and played with her in the dirt for an hour, and loved it! The distraction of my phone buzzing wasn't deterring my attention, and I could simply enjoy my daughter.

I was more in touch with my own emotions. I don't know if you're like me, but often my mind races fifty miles a minute. I multitask, while I'm multitasking, and am notorious for making lists. The default of being an incredible task tackler is that I'm often out of touch with my own emotions. Although I am very aware of others' emotions and feelings (I have to be, I'm prophetic), often I'm out of touch with my own. Self-reflection takes time, and also allowing myself to let go of my micromanagement of time.

The day I lost my phone, while my baby was taking a nap, I journaled for thirty minutes (without looking at the clock or being distracted by my phone). I processed with God my emotions, feelings, marriage, friendships, my own wants and needs, and what the Father thinks of me. It was amazing! I felt whole and at complete peace, all because I stopped, forgot about time, and became self-aware. I think self-aware people are dangerous to the enemy!

God stepped closer. No, not really. The truth is, I stepped closer to Him. By losing my phone and not being distracted to look at it all day, I felt His presence in a deeper measure. I found myself chatting with the Father and was able to hear Him much clearer. No phone. No distractions. Just being with Him.

So as my husband and I reflected that night on our day, and I shared with him how amazing it was to be disconnected from my phone, that's when it dawned on me. I, like most people in this generation, have a serious technology addiction. Here's the thing. In our society, phone addictions are mostly allowed. Our fast-paced society has bred a generation that is in need of constant, quick stimulation. Our attention span has shrunk immensely, as our technology has increased.

So, just how do we hear His still, quiet voice? We get still; we shrink down the other voices and distractions in our lives; we unplug; we get present, focusing on the here and now; and we develop the ability to patiently wait. And then, *He comes!*

4

Puddles

So, it was one of those incredibly difficult weeks. We've all had them. Those moments when we think, *What now, God?* And then BAM, something else attempts to strike us down! It started first on Sunday morning. My husband woke up early and had thought about going out to get me a surprise coffee. As he walked outside, he realized our car was gone! Our beautiful, practically new car, that someone had gifted to us when we returned to the States, was gone; stolen right off our driveway while we were soundly sleeping! Not the best way to start the week!

Later in the week, I had a scare with a German Shepherd dog running at me. Our sink backed up, and then our clothes dryer broke. Needless to say, all these things added up together in one week, rose my stress level.

I went to my in-law's house with a basket full of wet laundry. With that determination look in my eyes, I jumped out of our rental car (remember, our car was stolen!), baby in arms, and wondered, *How am I going to carry this basket and the baby downstairs to their dryer by myself?* But man I was determined. So I struggled but managed a supermom balancing act of baby and basket, and made it to the front door. Then it dawned on me, *Oh, no! I left the key to this house and my own house keys locked inside our house. All I have are these dumb rental car keys—and it's raining!*

Locked out in the rain! Quickly rethinking, *Well, at least we can jump back in the car where it's warm and drive to somewhere warm and walk around until my husband comes to the rescue with spare keys.* Then my toddler puts up a fight. Nope! Getting back in the car seat at this point, was not going to happen.

Fascinated by all the amazing puddles of water (her first-time experience with puddles), and leaves everywhere to smoosh, there was no deterring my daughter from playtime in the rain. *OK, I'll just roll with it,* I thought. So I led her to some puddles to jump in and out of, and piles of leaves to crunch. She was having the best day of her life! She would crunch a few leaves, but focus back on the puddles. After a while, I started thinking, *Why is she so obsessed with these puddles?*

And then I saw it. As I walked up to a puddle with her, suddenly the puddle changed colors. I saw heavenly colors move in the puddle. The water reflected back a multitude of colors that seemed to be alive. My little girl looked and smiled and laughed with glee!

"I'm inviting you in," I heard God say. "Come and taste My presence for a while, and leave your stress behind." I knew in that moment that God was inviting me to play, to experience Him, to see new things, and most of all to get refreshed.

So, my daughter and I played for thirty minutes in Heaven's puddles. We jumped and watched the colors change, and laughed together. It was a wonderful break for me from worrying about all the troubles life seemed to be throwing at us that week. Just to dip into His presence and laugh and enjoy Him. To lay down the cares of the world and just breathe in His peace and joy again. Ah, refreshed!

> *...In Your presence is fullness of joy; in Your right hand there are pleasures forever* (Psalm 16:11).

5

Reaching Out

THE MOST INCREDIBLE ENCOUNTERS I HAVE WITH GOD SEEM TO happen in the oddest, most unexpected places. It was a Thursday afternoon, and I was at the gym's pool trying to get back into my workout routine. It had been already more than ten days since I had thrown out my back. For a week I stayed mostly housebound—icing, stretching, essential oiling, etc.—everything I knew to do! Ever since having a baby, my back had never been the same. I kept praying for Jesus to heal my back, but didn't see any real improvement.

That morning when I woke up, I heard the Lord say, "Go swim some laps today." At first I was a little hesitant, thinking any physical activity could lead to more injury. But reluctantly, I got in the pool that day.

OK, Jesus. What are You up to, I thought as I dipped in. I began to swim, and in all honesty, kicking the water started increasing the pain in my back. As I swam lap after lap in pain, I finally ended up asking my Papa God, *God, do You remember me? Where are You?*

And just then, He answered my prayer. I encountered Him in the most unusual way. As I swam, I saw suddenly a Hand dip into the water in front of me, reach out, and grab my hand. It was so real to me in that moment that I really wondered if it was the lifeguard trying to pull me out of my lane for some reason.

But the Hand was warm, *really* warm! It also glowed with light behind it. I instantly heard His voice, "Ana, I'm reaching for you." I felt the warmth shoot from my right hand, all the way down my entire body, and rest on my lower back. Instant healing took place! Not only did my back get healed that day in the most unusual way, but my lane of the pool (and only my lane) also radiated light! There was no external light from the windows beaming into the pool that day. Nope! This was my Papa God! It was so extraordinarily odd that I got out of the pool to talk to the lifeguard about Jesus, prompted by his own curiosity of what was happening.

Sometimes, trials come at us in inopportune and uncomfortable ways—but in these moments He invites us in. He extends an invitation to us, "Will you reach out to Me and actually expect Me to respond?" The twelve days of pain I went through was such a trial. I prayed; I fasted; I sat asking my deep, unanswered questions before the King. Out of my discomfort, I found intimacy with Him. And then, and only then, did He reach out to me.

I've entered in, into this mysterious moment in my life when the King of all Glory is reaching down and connecting with me. I've always been able to connect with Him, but this season that I am in is different and like no other. We're reaching a new level of intimacy— me and God—and it amazes me each day. One thing I know for sure, I'm so happy I threw my back out. Through that trial of pain and suffering, I've been given victory and now access to step into a new level of intimacy with the King!

How is He reaching out to you today?

6

Pool of Presence

One day I had a vision that would help me keep my purpose. God spoke purpose over me through just a small encounter, but it has forever refreshed me, grounded me, and helped me understand how I can help bring people closer to the Father.

The pool before me brought such a refreshing peace as I bathed in it. Over and over as I splashed in it and each drop hit my face, His presence would come over me. The depth of His love was being poured over me, refreshing my spirit with the nature of Him. After I had drank deep of it, I turned and saw others beside me, looking with curiosity and a desire to come. So I led them to the pool, but they stood by the edge of the pool not knowing what to do. I showed them how to splash in the waters, how to pour the waters over their heads, and also hold it in their hands. Last, I showed them how to wash in His presence and renew their bodies, minds, and souls.

"Lead people here," I heard. "Bring people here. Usher them into the presence, and then show them how to wash in it. I'm bringing My refreshing presence to the Church. Times are coming when you will have to know how to tap into My presence and drink deeply to be restored. Bring them here, into the throne room, into My presence, and into the depth of My heart."

Psalm 65:4 says, *"How blessed is the one whom You choose and bring near to You to dwell in Your courts. We will be satisfied with the goodness of Your house, Your holy temple."*

7

Running Low

It was an early Tuesday morning, and surprisingly I was up before anyone else in the house. It's not unusual for me to be restless when I have something on my mind. I tossed and turned that night thinking with God about our current financial situation.

We had come into a dry season with my husband's website designing company, and business was at a low. I could feel despair and discouragement creeping into our house. That night before going to bed, my husband and I spent time praising and thanking God for what we did have, and declared financial breakthrough. This isn't our first time being without. After being missionaries overseas for years, we've both learned how to not let circumstances affect our faith and trust in the Father.

But, there I was...unable to reach deep sleep that night. So when I turned over and checked my phone and saw that it was finally a reasonable hour to go for a run, I was out the door in less than six minutes.

Running is like therapy for me. It's the one time the rest of the world seems to die down, my mind gets cleared, and all I can focus on are my strides and breathing. It started to rain that morning, which felt amazing! The humid air mixed with the cool raindrops falling on my head, felt like God was giving me a refreshing shower.

As I neared the end of my run, something shined light in my eyes from the side of the road and caught my attention. I picked up a shiny nickel from the road. Most people would think, *So what, it's just five cents,* but not me in that moment. See, I love to collect coins and fill my piggy bank even though I am a grown adult. When that piggy gets full, I enjoy emptying it and giving the money to a charity. So seeing the nickel, I got excited.

I picked it up, and that's when I heard Him. God's voice rang through my head, "Financial breakthrough coming. I have not forgotten you." Instantly, I was reminded of my own smallness and how awesome my God is. In an instant He spoke into the gaping place in my heart; He spoke into the very place the enemy was trying to prod my family—will you trust Him?

For some odd reason, I felt in my heart the need to give the nickel back to the Lord. It was just five cents, but to me in that moment, it meant so much more. It was a small simple, "Yes, Lord. I trust You and know You will always take care of us. This is Yours and I give it back to You."

So I looked for somewhere to sow it. The biblical principal "You reap what you sow," flashed through my mind as I looked for a place to drop the nickel. I saw a giant puddle that actually seemed like a good place. Running by, I dropped it in. Taking two strides more, I looked down and there in front of me was another shiny new nickel. I picked it up with tears in my eyes and heard the Father's voice saying, "As you give your life and sow into My Kingdom, you will always have more than enough."

8

Rain of Presence

"If I give it all to you, will you make it all new? If I open up my hands, will you fill them again?" Will Reagan and the United Pursuit band blared through my earphones, and it was 3 in the morning. Some of my best Jesus times and encounters happen at 3 A.M. All I can do is describe what I see, and where I went.

I saw it. The curtain that had once shown up in our living room; a curtain of the Lord's presence returned. This same curtain had once come to our living room and stayed hovering for two weeks. During that time, people rolled through our house to encounter His presence. What a glorious time that was. Healing broke out those two weeks, and refreshing, heartfelt encounters were experienced.

Tonight, the curtain appeared and glistened with raindrops falling down, and I knew the Lord was here. All I could do was lay back my head under the thick weight of His glory and surrender to the moment. His presence came like a sweet, refreshing, and much-needed kiss. The Father, the King of Glory was touching down and deciding to rest in my living room again. Why, I don't know, but who cares really in that moment!

All I could see around me was a blanket of rain dripping down. The curtain dripped with it, the ceiling dripped with it, and my feet dipped in the water that was now a couple of inches deep.

As I laid my head back under His sweet presence, suddenly I saw myself in another place. I was outside getting drenched by the rain. I looked around and saw my angel standing to the left of me and Holy Spirit to the right. We all laughed and opened our arms to catch the rain drops. I looked up, and saw just for a second the Father's eyes looking down on me. I heard His voice then say, "Find Me in the storm."

That's it. Simple but profound as I stood there, head back and arms outstretched, soaking in His presence. Suddenly joy overtook me, and I started laughing. Holy Spirit and my angel also must have felt it as they started laughing too. We laughed and laughed for what seemed like forever, in His presence, in that sweet, warm rain of His glory.

And then back I was in my living room.

Where did I forget His presence, I asked myself. In the busyness of life, and trust me, it's crazy busy right now— I missed these moments. These sweet moments of laying it all down and just capturing His sweet presence. Even my time studying the Word had become dry.

But here I was now, water still dripping down my back, renewed again. There must be a way, a way to not lose that focus. I'm reminded of my daughter. Sometimes in group settings, she'll catch my eye from across the room, and nothing can deter her look for me. That look melts me, and I'm sure our heavenly Father feels the same; when in the midst of it all, when the storms are pouring down, we lay our heads back, and look to Him.

9

Be Peace

THERE I WAS. IT HAD BEEN A HEAVY WEEK, INTENSE POURING OUT OF ministry, and I finally had a moment to myself. The kids were both taking their naps, and I had a moment to just breathe.

I sat with my cup of coffee freshly made, worship music plugged into my ears, and had the inner dialog that Jesus and I have so often, "God, if You would like to take me up and show me something new in Heaven today, that would be awesome. Just saying…" And I waited. Having encounters and experiencing Heaven regularly has been a gift God has given me, but here I was experiencing *nothing!* No encounter! I thought, *What am I doing wrong? Should I be praying more, should I be worshiping louder?*

"Just *be,* Ana," I heard the Lord respond. "Take time for you. Enjoy the sun!"

OK, I thought. So I got out the new *Magnolia Journal* magazine— which I never have time to read these days. As I was enjoying my coffee, sunshine, and flipping through the pages, I came across an article that struck me. Joanna Gains wrote: "But when I do choose simplicity and keep choosing it in whatever ways matter to me, I am different. I have room to breathe. I have space to see clearly.…"

Now granted she was writing about spring cleaning, but Holy Spirit kept highlighting the phrase to me, "I have room to breathe. I have space to see clearly."

"Shut your eyes, Ana. Turn off your music, and be still," I heard.

So I did just that, and then *boom,* just like that, I was up in an out-of-body experience. This time in Heaven was much different and unlike others I have experienced before. This one stands apart.

All around me, all I could see was empty, white space. No floor, no ceiling. Just me walking in empty, white space. There was a warmth and stillness unlike anything I have ever experienced. I walked around in it for a little bit, admittedly alarmed. *Am I not seeing, God?* I thought. *Aren't You going to show me more?* Most of my Heaven encounters are so vivid, and the atmosphere is almost electric in some of them, that this felt so uncomfortably different. Vast nothing. Empty, white space.

Then a large hand came and gently took hold of my hand. It was the Father's hand. All I was allowed to see was His hand holding mine, in this vast, empty, white space.

Finally, He spoke, "Ana, Ana, you are used to praying for peace from the wrong perspective. I want you to learn that My peace is not about just an atmospheric state or shift, but rather a state of being. I am the Prince of Peace. I am in you. I have given you the gift of peace.

It's yours now to be. Claim it as yours."

A real change happened for me that day. No longer do I see peace as something far off that I have to work for to gain in the midst of my busy schedule, but rather, I carry peace within me. It's already mine to claim. It's up to me now just to live it out.

Peace is not determined by circumstance. In this day and age, we have to be the Body of Christ that is truly rooted and grounded in Him. We know who we are, despite what our circumstances throw our way. If *Christ is truly in us, the hope of all glory* (Col. 1:27), we have to look and smell different. Are we radiating the fragrance of Christ in the midst of everything that is going on in the world? Are we tapping into the peace that surpasses all understanding (Phil. 4:7)? When we truly grasp our inheritance as sons and daughters of Christ, a transformation occurs. There is a crossover from trying to grasp on to God and trying to hold on to Him, to understanding that we have the living God inside of us!

> *Blessed are the peacemakers, for they will be called children of God* (Matthew 5:9 NIV).

10

Joy, Expectation, and Belief

PERHAPS, ONE OF THE MOST CHALLENGING AND ALSO FREEING SCRIPtures in the Word of God is *"Unless you are converted and become like children, you will not enter the kingdom of heaven"* (Matt. 18:3). For those of us who have maturity on our side, and a few years under our belt, what exactly does that look like? With the daily responsibilities of "life"—work, family, kids, finances, relationships, health, etc., how do we maintain our childlike nature?

You know one thing I love about children? They don't hold back! They say whatever is on their mind—unreserved. I remember a few times when my daughter has said things out loud (bless her sweetness), that left me in shock. One time we were at a park, and another mom was shouting at her child and losing her temper completely. Veera (my daughter who was 3 at the time), came to me and said very loudly, "Mommy, that mommy needs a spanking. She's shouting at that boy. She needs a time out. That's not nice!" Oh my! If only you could see my face in that moment! I was speechless, at first.

Entering into God's presence as a child is one of the hardest accomplishments for some of us. We have our reservations. Times in the past when we allowed our guards down, we've been hurt or burnt. Or maybe we grew up in a family where being reserved, controlled, or held back was a norm. Or maybe our culture even honors holding feeling and emotions in. Whatever it may be, life happens and we lose our ability to enter in as children.

Healthy children who are loved, and know they are loved, ask for what they want. Like David dancing without reservation before the ark of the covenant (2 Sam. 6), or Moses crying out to God, *"Now show me your glory!"* (Exod. 33:18 NIV), children don't hold back.

But as adults, we forget how to be children in faith. We forget how to just believe wholeheartedly; to ask directly for what we want from God. We stop sharing with God our raw emotions, wrongly thinking that maybe it's just too much for Him to handle. We forget how to just simply *be* with God, and not desire anything from Him, but just sit in His lap, look up into His eyes, and see His smiling eyes gazing back at ours. And, we forget how to walk in our own mantles and callings that God has birthed in us from the beginning of time.

I had a vision one day of me playing with a giant string. I was dipping it into soapy water and then pulling it back out to make an enormous bubble. Then I had an idea to jump into the bubble, and was surprised when it didn't pop. Instead, the bubble engulfed me, and I found myself inside it looking out. Then I heard, "It's that easy. With childlike joy and My presence around you, you will jump into this next season. Have joy, expectation, and belief!"

With childlike joy, expectation, and belief, the enemy cannot hold us back! I call it the "triple threat"! We believe our Papa Daddy is bigger, stronger, and greater than any weapon formed against us from the enemy. We are bold and courageous and full of faith. And we run and take risks, knowing that God is with us and for us. We seek Him wholeheartedly and get filled up with His presence, making us unstoppable.

So today, would you choose to enter in as a child? Would you choose to take a moment and picture yourself sitting in your loving, heavenly Father's lap, and let Him love on you. Let Him speak to you, and you yourself carry no other agenda than to simply be with Him.

11

Co-Laborers

HAVE YOU EVER HAD A DREAM THAT YOU KNEW WAS FROM THE LORD, but had no idea what it meant at first? Well, that happened to me. In typical God form (or at least that's how God and me roll), He gave me the most incredible dream, with no explanation, and left me hanging, waiting for Him to give me the interpretation.

This is often my relationship with God and Holy Spirit. I'll have a dream or encounter, and not always understand it at first. In His lovingkindness, God then brings other people along who prophesy into what He had shown me—not even knowing they are giving me the revelation I had been waiting for. (That's why I write down all my God encounters, so I can always go back and reread them and declare them over myself and my family when I have understanding.)

There I was in my dream with Holy Spirit. God always presents Holy Spirit to me in the form of a woman, actually. Every time this woman shows up in my dreams, I know she represents to me Holy Spirit. So there my Best Friend, Holy Spirit, and I were, wearing lab coats and standing at a counter lined with petri dishes. We were in a chemistry lab performing experiments. I looked on the counter and there were four petri dishes with clear liquid in them.

Holy Spirit looked at me with a twinkle in her eye (like playfully saying, I dare you), and handed me a dropper full of liquid. As I dropped a few drops into a dish, the color changed from clear to a vibrant purple. Then Holy Spirit dropped one drop on top of mine and the color completely transformed to a vibrant orange. We both laughed, and then the two of us just kept dropping colors together, just to see what new colors would emerge from the dishes.

I woke up and thought, *What in the world was that about, Lord?*

For two days, I mulled it over in my mind. What was God trying to show me? What was He trying to teach me? Then a prophetic friend came for a visit and randomly dropped the revelation I'd been waiting for. "Ana," he said, "You are in a season of co-laboring with Holy Spirit right now." As soon as he said it, I knew that was right. I felt it in my spirit that was the Word of the Lord—co-laboring!

Isn't it truly amazing that we get to co-labor with Christ! In Luke chapter 9, the disciples had the opportunity to be co-laborers. The disciples responded to a problem they saw, telling Jesus, *"'Send the crowd away, that they may go into the surrounding villages and countryside and find lodging and get something to eat; for here we are in a desolate place.' But He said to them, 'You give them something to eat!'"* (Luke 9:12-13). After this, the disciples witnessed the food multiplication miracle—where the little amount of food they had was multiplied to feed the crowds. I'm sure it blew them away!

There are seasons we go through when we pray, "God, please do this…." Then there are other seasons God puts us in where He extends an invitation and asks us, "You do your part, and I'll do Mine." We get to co-labor with Him!

What's God putting in your heart to do today with Him? What's your part?

12

Bethesda Pool

I USED TO ALWAYS READ JOHN CHAPTER 5 AS IF IT ONLY RELATED TO healing. As I have been in healing ministry for quite some time now, it became so easy for me to relate this Scripture and teach from it as how to pray for someone who has been sick for quite some time or chronically ill.

But then God shook me up today. As the man at the pool of Bethesda sat day in and day out waiting for the "moving of the waters," in which the Angel of the Lord would release healing to those who first got in the pool, I heard the Lord say, "Ana, you're right there. You're right there on that mat beside the pool waiting for My Spirit to move, as if it's not tangible for you."

What! No I'm not, Lord, I thought. *I'm not waiting for a healing. I've already been healed by Your stripes.*

"No, Ana. You're not getting it. You are like him. It's how you're operating in ministry. Are you aware that I have the best for you, and it's available to you at all times? Do you move and act as if you are a daughter of the King, and everything, yes *everything* is available to you? Or are you really operating out of an orphan spirit most of the time, waiting and hoping that My Spirit will move? Claim what is readily yours already and walk with confidence."

"Jesus said to him, 'Get up, pick up your pallet and walk'" (John 5:8).

Ouch. In that moment, God pulled back layers of my heart, revealing areas of my life where I still lacked faith. I have worked with orphans before in my time overseas, and a common feeling they all have is that they don't expect good things to happen to them. When I've seen children break away from the orphan spirit that has so haunted them their whole lives, and really start to step into their identity as royal sons or daughters of the King—wow! What a change! The expectation and belief that their Papa Daddy will do what His Word says is obvious!

But there I was. In my own way, even after years of having a relationship with the King, even after time after time of watching and partnering with Jesus to do miracles in my own life and others' lives, I was still not feeling good enough, and still not believing in God to do some of the impossible blessings and promises He has told me He will do—and feeling like an orphan child.

We all know it: *"The thief comes only to steal and kill and destroy"* (John 10:10). So, where has the enemy possibly come in and stolen your own belief in the good things the King has for you today? Is there any area of your life and ministry, that you are not walking in confidence? Is there any door that seems locked shut in your life, that you are just waiting for the Lord to open?

Oh that I would know Your glory, God, and claim it as mine today.

13

Fragrance and Presence

THERE HE WAS. JUST LIKE THAT, I FOUND MYSELF TRAILING BEHIND Jesus. The ends of His robe kicked up as we walked through the rows of flowers, and I tried to grab on. We were in The Garden. Often, Jesus has taken me up into His Garden to teach me new qualities about His character. He looked back at me with that mysterious smile that I have grown to love. "Come follow Me," He said.

I watched as He walked in between the two rows of roses. His hands would gently stroke past each flower, and I watched as the flowers responded to His presence. It's like I could see them taking in a breath of Him as He touched each one, and then they would exhale their sweet aroma and stretch upward.

He took his time, caring for His flowers; stopping at a few to admire them, or prune a few here and there. Meanwhile, I grabbed onto the end tips of his robe. *If God's giving me this opportunity to be here in this Garden walking with Him, then I'm going to grab onto all of Him that I can,* I thought.

Then He stopped. "I want you to look at this, Ana," Jesus said. I looked and I saw in the palm of His hand a small rose. I'm no flower expert (like my mom), but the color was a very unusual blue for a rose. The color was similar to a bluish purple, like a vibrant periwinkle.

"Rub the petals, Ana," He instructed me. As I did, the outer petals started to rub off their oils onto my fingertips. "These flowers and petals carry My healing of peace on them. Carry My fragrance back with you, Ana."

Then just like that, I was out of the encounter and back in the sanctuary of our church during a worship service, right before I was about to head back to brief our healing teams for the night. When I looked at my left hand, my fingertips and palm had oil on them. Not dripping oil, but the palm and tips that had touched the petals were wet, where the other hand was not.

What an unusual experience, I thought as I went into the side room. Later, God revealed to me that this fragrance of peace that had rubbed off on me was something I was to carry to the next place I planned to minister. "Bring My peace," was the phrase I kept being reminded of as I packed and planned to pour out at an upcoming conference.

Wouldn't you know, the week before the trip, I felt anything but peace. My family was hit with spiritual warfare on all sides—kids sick, marriage miscommunications, and stressful new twists in the days leading up to the trip to throw me off. Clearly my Papa Daddy knew what I myself needed to have first before I went to minister.

Can you imagine what it was like to walk with God in The Garden every day? I imagine it was peaceful; I imagine it was joyful; I imagine it was a very creative environment. Can you see yourself now with Him? Can you imagine yourself walking with Him in The Garden? Try and catch the end of the train of His robe. Grab onto His peace today.

For we are a fragrance of Christ to God among those who are being saved and among those who are perishing (2 Corinthians 2:15).

14

Dream Big

I WILL NEVER FORGET WHEN GOD DID A HUGE MIRACLE FOR MY HUS-
band and me. We had just returned from being missionaries overseas
in Nepal and India. We had literally no money, no job, and no understanding or direction from the Lord as to why we came back from
overseas.

Talk about a challenging time! God had told us to come back, with
no further explanation. Obediently, we packed our bags and jumped
on planes to head home.

There we found ourselves in the middle of the United States with
no way to get around. So we started to pray. "Lord, we need a car, or
the money to be able to purchase a car." We kept praying, without
much direction or hope.

Then one day I heard His voice. "Ana, ask Me specifically for the
type of car you want. Call it in, but be specific. What do you want,
Ana?"

At first that kind of blew me away. "What do I want!" A poverty
spirit had been so ingrained in me from living overseas with hardly
ever anything, that the concept of being able to ask God for what I
wanted, stretched me.

So I started to think for a bit, and then it came to mind. "Well, God," I said, "I guess I would like a car that is a little spacious so that we could put future baby seats in it, higher up so that I can see (since I'm a little person), functioning air conditioning and heat now that we live back in the Midwest where there are real seasons, and could You let it not be a car from the 1990s but rather made in the 2000s? And one more thing, God, could You give us a car that's from the little old lady who never drives anywhere so the car will have low mileage but be in new condition?"

So, I made this prayer request, which at the time I thought would be absolutely impossible for God. Do you know what He did? He gave us a car! The car was exactly as I described—from the little old lady who hardly ever drove, under 30,000 miles on it, a 2000-something Scion, had air conditioning and a heater and is super spacious.

With that gift, God really wrecked my notion of the Scripture that says ask and you shall receive (see Matt. 7:7). Up until then, I knew there was power in my prayers. I have seen plenty of miracles and breakthrough when seeing people receive prayer, but this was different. I'll never forget those feelings I had when we went and picked up our new, free car. *Wow! God, You really do love me and care for me! You really care.*

Sometimes, life beats us up. We don't get the breakthrough right away that we are seeking. We experience hurt in our hearts from broken relationships. We forget that God really does care.

Do you know your Father cares for you today? Do you know that He loves to shower His blessings on His children? I just pray that you, today, would experience the generosity and love of the Father. Go with boldness to the Father and ask Him for what you need. Believe and know that the Lord is good and loves to bless you. Declare what it is you want to see God do, and then claim it as yours.

15

Gates

Open to me the gates of righteousness; I shall enter through them, I shall give thanks to the Lord. This is the gate of the Lord; the righteous will enter through it (Psalm 118:19-20).

Enter His gates with thanksgiving and His courts with praise. Give thanks to Him, bless His name (Psalm 100:4).

EVER HAVE ONE OF THOSE DAYS WHEN YOU DON'T FEEL THE FULLNESS of the joy of the Lord? When praising God seems like the last thing you want to do? Well, I was having one of those days. I had just returned from a very fruitful ministry trip. I had poured out my heart and ministered with everything I could, and God had moved in such incredible ways. Our team saw people physically healed, emotionally healed, filled up with the power and loving touch of God, angels released and ministering, and more. It really was an incredible weekend of huge breakthrough!

And then I returned home. I returned to find my daughter had a cough that had developed into the croup, my baby boy had bronchiolitis and was also super sick, and my husband was exhausted from

35

taking care of sick kids while I was gone. After praying over my kids that morning and then rushing them to the doctor to have them examined in the urgent care, I returned home that afternoon and no part of me felt like praising God.

"Why, God? WHY?" was my conversation with God. "Why did they get sick while I was gone? Why does the enemy hit my family hard when I am out ministering? Why do I see people healed right and left by Your power, and yet my own children are sick now?" My list of complaints and lamentations went on and on to God.

"Ana, just praise Me. It's going to be OK, but just stop. Stop right now and seek My face in the midst of it all. Feel My peace; praise My name. Release praise as your weapon," I heard the voice of the Lord say.

Now I know that praise and thanksgiving are the keys to enter into His presence. So I set down my list of complaints and began to praise God. I thanked Him for all that He is and all that He is doing in my life. I praised Him for His faithfulness, goodness, and lovingkindness. You know what happened? Once I started, I didn't want to stop praising Him. Before I knew it, thirty minutes had already passed that I had spent thanking and praising Him.

Then I saw a shift happen. In the spirit I saw a vision of a little gate being swung wide open for me, and then His presence came. I saw His presence come and fill my house; slowly at first, and then it became thicker and thicker. Defeat was no longer dwelling in my house. It had to make way and take a hike as His presence came crashing in. No longer did I feel defeated. No longer did I feel my frustrations. I felt His complete peace and joy, despite my circumstances.

Will you praise Him today? Will you build up your weaponry muscles and give Him thanksgiving, despite what you may feel? Watch the enemy run as you enter in His gates with thanksgiving and praise!

16

A Room for You
in Heaven

EVER HAVE ONE OF THOSE DAYS? THAT DAY WHEN EVERYTHING THAT could go wrong does. *Is something against me?* you might find yourself asking. Thing upon thing compounds to make you wonder, *Will I even make it through this horrendous day?*

Well, I was having one of those days. I woke up to the sound of my daughter not able to breathe. Her little cough had grown unbearable, and she had kept us up coughing throughout the entire night. I looked at the clock—2 A.M.! *OK, I got this,* I thought to myself. I rolled out of bed and cranked up the shower so steam would fill the bathroom. My daughter and I sat in the bathroom, snacking on raisins, breathing in the steam. Didn't work—still coughing!

OK, I got this, I thought again. We put on every layer we could think of and headed outside into the 22-degree weather. Her pediatrician had told me that breathing in the cold air would actually be good for her cough. So together we took a lovely, frigid tour of the neighborhood at now, 3 A.M. Still, the cough pressed on.

At 5 A.M., we ended up in the hospital, with my daughter receiving a breathing treatment and oral steroids. Finally, we made it back home around 7 A.M. I won't go into the details about the rest of the start of my day, but to summarize there was an accidental mascara incident—and my eye puffed up nicely for the rest of the day!

When the kids went to sleep, Jesus and I met. "God, I need You," I cried out to Him. "Please come fill me up, because I got nothing left for this day," I begged.

Then, just like that, I was walking with Jesus down a long corridor in Heaven. To my surprise I saw a new door, a turquoise door. I was instantly attracted to it—turquoise being my favorite color. "What's that door," I asked. "It's your door," Jesus said back to me with a smile and twinkle in His eye. "Like, that's my personal door? That's my room?" I asked excitedly. "Let's just go have a look," He responded.

Together we opened the exquisite door, and there I discovered many hobby stations set up in the room—ones that bring me joy. Jesus led me to a large canvas that was on an easel. Together we picked up paintbrushes and began to paint on the giant piece. Colors came together and what came out of our masterpiece was a picture of the ocean. As I started staring at the waves of the sea, I suddenly found myself *in* the picture. I was walking on the shoreline of the beach, staring at the crashing ocean waves. I could feel the warmth and squishy sand between my toes. I felt a wave of sadness come over me though. I was walking alone. "Why am I so alone God?" I asked sadly.

"But you're not," said a voice behind me. I turned around, and there right behind me was the Lion of Judah. His very presence took me aback. He had been walking behind me the entire time. We walked along together then; I held on to His mane.

"I am always with you. Always," He said. Then I danced in the sand and kicked it up in the air. I felt my joy restored.

As I came out of this encounter and sat pondering it, I thought, *Isn't that just amazing?! God cares enough about me to set up a special* room in Heaven that's just for me; full of the hobbies and treasures that bring me joy.

God cares about you too. He knows what you need in this very moment and is with you. You are not alone.

> Let his left hand be under my head and his right hand embrace me (Song of Solomon 2:6).

17

Thorn Plucking

Ooooo, ouch that hurt! Has someone you love ever said something that feels like it cuts to the core of your being and smashes it to pieces? OK, OK. I know I'm being a little melodramatic here, but isn't it funny how the people closest to us can sometimes hurt us the worst?

The Scripture in Proverbs comes to mind, *"Death and life are in the power of the tongue..."* (Prov. 18:21). Well, I was having one of those deathly feeling moments. I'm not going to hash it out here and explain what was said (it's old water under the bridge now), but let's just say the enemy really used someone's words and twisted them to hurt me to the core.

Now I know what you're thinking, *But, wait. You get hurt?* You know what, I'm just like anyone else. I have feelings, and those get hurt sometimes. But God's given me a little wisdom on how to deal with hurt feelings that I'd like to share.

So there I was; completely feeling smushed and crushed by someone I deeply cared about. I had already forgiven the person, but the wound was still open. I was dwelling on what was said, revisiting the conversation in my mind (am I the only one who does this?), and Jesus paid me a visit.

"Come with Me," He said. He took me to an open clearing, looked me square in the eye, and asked me, "Are you ready to give over your wound and give it back to Me?"

I thought about it for a second, and then nodded yes.

Then I felt the mighty hand of God come and reach inside of me. He plucked a thorn out of my heart, and I'm not going to lie, the process really did hurt. It hurt at first, but then it actually felt really good; it almost felt relieving, as if a splinter had been plucked out and the built-up pressure was now released. Then He planted a rose in its place.

"It will still have thorns on it, and will need pruning occasionally, but it will be easier now and will smell sweet," Jesus pointed out to me.

And just like that, I was back in my kitchen where I had been mulling over that conversation in the first place. My heart still felt a little ache, but it felt much better than it did before.

God delivered me that day of a festering wound. He delivered me from the enemy's twists and manipulation of what was said to cause me further injury. The enemy not only takes hurtful words spoken to us or over us and uses them as trap doors to get in and corrupt us with anger, bitterness, unforgiveness, or confusion, he also tries to use them to create in us wrong beliefs about ourselves. I had forgiven that person, but a wrongful word that was said, created in me a wrong belief. I had come into agreement about myself with that belief, which left the wound wide open for the enemy's attacks.

But the Lord heals our wounds, helps us break off wrong agreements, helps us forgive, and gives us guidance how to nurture our relationships in the future.

The relationship I have with that person, to this day, is just like the Lord showed me. It sometimes needs pruning and clipping to help it along, but it grows more and more beautiful each year. And the wound is no longer there.

So today, is there any wound you might be carrying in your heart that the Lord needs to come pluck out of you? Will you have the courage to give it to Him?

18

Believe Again

I saw the most incredible presence of the Lord and angels all around me one day. His presence was so tangible that I could feel tingling happening throughout my body. Angelic wings brushed past my face and skin. The wind of the Holy Spirit moved throughout the room.

And then I heard His voice. "I'm going to restore your belief. Your belief in the impossible has diminished. Somewhere, somehow you've lost it. Your hope and belief for your own life has grown dim. You have faith for others, but for your own dreams your faith and belief has lessened. Get ready! I'm about to do the impossible. "

Then with my eyes closed, I saw a picture of a light. It was foggy and far away, but then I saw it grow closer, and more clear and strong. It became bright again.

Has life diminished your belief? I know God will speak to readers through what I'm sharing in this book—perhaps He's speaking to you right now. I can feel His presence even as I type these words.

Maybe you need to know right now that *God is* going to move that mountain of impossibility. Maybe things have happened in your life to diminish your own belief in dreams you once had—but I'm telling you today, believe again! Pick up your dreams and present them to God—He's the God of impossibility!

> *Peter said to Him, "Lord, if it is You, command me to come to You on the water." And He said, "Come!" And Peter got out of the boat, and walked on the water and came toward Jesus. But seeing the wind, he became frightened, and beginning to sink, he cried out, "Lord, save me!" Immediately Jesus stretched out His hand and took hold of him, and said to him, "You of little faith, why did you doubt?"* (Matthew 14:28-31)

Peter's situation, and what Peter saw in the natural caused him to start sinking. You see, he started losing faith and belief when he saw those ginormous waves. It is key where we set our focus. Do we focus on the mountain, or are we focusing on Jesus pulling us up every mountain standing before us?

Do you have faith to dream something that would be completely impossible for you to ever reach on your own? Do you have faith to ask God for the impossible?

I'll never understand how God intertwines the happenings of my life to create the most beautiful mosaic. But I trust Him. I trust Him with the core of my being; He is good; He is for me not against me; and although I can't always understand the way He works, He always is in control.

Believe again? Will you trust Him today?

19

Pick Your Position

ONE DAY, AT THE START OF MY DAY WITH THE LORD, HE TOOK ME soaring. Over an hour and a half passed, and I was completely having encounter after encounter with the Lord.

It started with a vision where I saw myself soaring over a landscape with Jesus. As I soared closer, He showed me a battlefield. I could see hundreds upon thousands of people fighting in a battle against demonic, oppressive spirits. They were all on the ground fighting from a position of defense. The oppressive spirits were bigger and stronger than each one of the people, and the people were losing. Then I saw the King of Glory, Jesus Himself, dressed in His royal robes, ride up on a huge white horse. "Rise up!" He commanded the people. Suddenly horses appeared for every person on the field, and I saw the people mount the horses and dressed in completely new armor. They were ready to do and win this battle.

When I had this vision, I was going through a rough time in my pregnancy. I was secretly struggling with so much self-doubt, and didn't even know how to tell anyone about it. I kept it a secret from the world. My own husband didn't even know. In my times with the Lord, I would cry out to Him to reveal why I was experiencing this and to take it from me. I knew it wasn't my portion. Many medical doctors had told me that during pregnancy I would experience hormonal waves and inconsistencies in my emotions. I didn't want to agree with that, but yet here I was going through it. *Have I failed God?* I thought to myself. *Is there something wrong with me?* I wondered.

Then I had that vision of the battlefield. After the vision, I heard the Lord's voice saying to me, "You are not under the curse, but above it. Find your weaponry, for you have lost it."

So, I started to think, *What is my weaponry of choice?* Instantly, I remembered the phrase, "The joy of the Lord is my strength." I started declaring it over myself: "The joy of the Lord is my strength! The joy of the Lord is my strength! The joy, of the Lord, is my strength!" The more and more I said it, the more and more I could feel the heaviness of self-doubt lift off me. This gave me encouragement to keep going! "No weapon formed against me shall prosper, in Jesus' name I declare! Self-doubt, you must now leave! I am covered in the blood of the lamb, and you have no power here anymore!"

Do you know what happened? That self-doubt I was feeling, it left. It left, and it never came back! So many of us are picking a battle from a position of defeat. We are victims of the enemy's attacks. We agree that this is our portion; this is just what we have to go through. So many times the emphasis on the first part of John 10:10 is brought to attention, but less on the second part: *"The thief comes only to steal and kill and destroy; I came that they may have life and have it abundantly."* Jesus came that we may have life and live it abundantly!

So, are you living? You are not defeated. Rise up. Rise up, oh Church, and let us claim our victorious positions.

46

20

Breaking Out From Performance

THE CURTAINS STARTED MOVING AND I HEARD HIS VOICE. IT WASN'T the first time He had taken me through these royal, purple curtains into His presence, and it certainly wouldn't be the last. Just prior to this encounter with Jesus, I had made a simple prayer, "Lord, would You take me up? I need a fresh encounter with Your presence today."

Then I saw the curtains. With my eyes closed, I saw the imagery of giant purple curtains moving, as if there was something behind them waiting for me. The soft fabric glided across my face, and I could feel warmth there. I heard the voice, "Enter in," He said.

There I came face to face with Jesus on the other side of the curtains. He looked at me and smiled. Energy and radiance came through those eyes. I've never seen eyes that look so alive, except for in the face of Jesus. I immediately started pouring out my heart to Jesus, as I would a friend. I told Him how I thought I should be doing more for Him ministerial wise; that I felt like I wasn't doing enough for Him.

"Ana, Ana," He stopped me. "When are you going to break out from under that performance spirit?"

I shut my eyes and realized that I was indeed feeling the need to perform for Jesus. I had come under the need to prove myself to God without even realizing it. Here I had sat through countless preachings or teachings about "performance spirit," and yet I had never realized I was operating in it in my own relationship with the Father. I felt the need to perform even in my relationship with God.

With my eyes still shut, I then heard the phrase "Behold, breathe, and experience Me," so I invited the presence of the Lord to come and renew me. I stopped the rumble of thoughts pouring through my head, just to sit and be still and breathe.

Then His presence came. It was small at first, but then I felt Him come stronger and stronger. Soon God's presence was so strongly hovering over me that I had to lie down and rest under it. The need to perform for God felt so silly now compared to the magnitude of His weighty presence hanging over me.

"I renounce it," I heard myself say. "I renounce this performance spirit in Jesus' name, and command it to go. It can't enter into my relationship with You, God, anymore."

Instantly I felt the peace of the Lord walk into the room and enter my spirit. No longer did I feel uncomfortable sitting under that weighty presence, but rather felt absolute peace and ability to rest under it and just receive. To just breathe.

The Lord bless you, and keep you; the Lord make His face shine on you, and be gracious to you; the Lord lift up His countenance on you and give you peace (Numbers 6:24-26).

21

Pour Out

THERE ARE MANY TIMES WHEN THE LORD HAS TAKEN ME UP INTO Heaven and allowed me to sit with Him at the Father's table and partake. I've eaten some of the most exquisite food there, unlike anything I have ever tasted on earth. I've learned so many different lessons from God at that table, it has become one of my favorite places to go with Jesus.

One time, my role at the banquet table was different. I was in a vision and saw myself at the table. Instead of partaking and eating this time, I was setting out all the fruit at the appropriate places. And I was going around ahead of the meal making sure all the silverware was laid out for the banquet.

As I walked around the room, I heard Him say to me, "You've tasted well My presence. Now it's time for you to prepare to bring other people here."

There have been seasons in my life when God asks me to just rest under His presence and receive. There are also seasons, though, when God calls me, and you, to pour out. We can't just be sponges basking in His glory all day without letting some of the glory squeeze out and splash onto people in our lives.

The more we behold Him, the more we start mirroring Him. There is a pattern that reflects this principle. As we can see from Scripture, Moses would go up the mountain and spend time in the glorious presence of God, so much so that his own face would actually shine with God's glory.

> But whenever he entered the Lord's presence to speak with him, he removed the veil until he came out. And when he came out and told the Israelites what he had been commanded, they saw that his face was radiant. Then Moses would put the veil back over his face until he went in to speak with the Lord (Exodus 34:34-35 NIV).

Moses would then come down the mountain and pour out the knowledge that he had received from God for the people of Israel. Soak in and pour out; soak in and pour out. It's a rhythm of Heaven. Receive and give it out. Receive and give it out. To whom He gives more, He requires more—and it's our joy to give it.

I never get tired of telling people about the goodness of God and riches of Heaven that I have experienced. The more I share, the more people will encounter it themselves.

So what's your portion today? Where is your realm of influence? Who are you involved with day in and day out who needs you to pour into them the love of Christ?

People ask me all the time, "How can I move in the prophetic more? How can I have the gifts?" My answer is simple, "Love God, get full of Him, and then *go and love people*. Serve them, and watch what God will do.

22

Lean In

I woke up today feeling sick. My body was sending me a sign, a sign that it was time to rest and step back from a few too many activities and allow my body to restore itself. My throat throughout the day was sore; my voice was scratchy. I just kept going. With two little ones at home, laundry seems endless. *I gotta keep going. I just can't rest,* I thought. I know I'm not alone in this crazy, bizarre type of thinking. I mean, what crazy animals would keep driving themselves into the ground when they are sick or injured? Humans, that's who!

Later it was ministry night for me at the church. As the associate director of the healing rooms, Tuesday nights are go times for me and my family. I arrive early to help setup, then I walk around the room and prayerfully shift the atmosphere and invite the presence of God into the room. I make sure every team member has everything they need. I make sure the worship team and sound system is going smoothly. I go over the flow of the night with the other directors of our healing rooms, and ask Jesus for direction.

My throat kept hurting. The more I talked, the more it ached. Unconsciously, I kept rubbing my neck where my tonsils are. "Go lie down, Ana," I heard the voice of the Lord command me. So I did just that. In the sanctuary where the live worship was happening, I stretched out on a back row of chairs so as not to be a distraction. I raised my hands to the sky worshiping God. (I must have looked quite odd, but when I'm going after God, hey, who cares what I look like!)

As I stretched my hands up, I suddenly saw a picture. I saw Jesus in an instance. He looked at me, grabbed onto my hands, and blew in my face. This wasn't like a soft, gentle wind. Oh no! It was a mighty wind that sent tingles all the way down my body. It shook me to the core. The breath of God was being poured over me. I noticed then that my throat was no longer hurting. God gave me the strength I needed in that moment to minister and pour out on people who were coming for prayer and also to my team.

I learned two things tonight. Number one: it's OK and necessary to take a step back, lie down, and rightfully so, to take care of myself. God doesn't want slaves, but lovers. Sometimes we can work ourselves too much, forgetting that God values the person over what we can do.

Number two: I've learned in moments of weakness to lean into God. Time and time again I've leaned onto His chest and asked Him, "So God, what do You have to say about this? Please come touch me." Let's not be afraid to lean into God when we need it. He's big enough. He can handle it!

The disciple that Jesus dearly loved was at the right of him at the table and was leaning his head on Jesus (John 13:23 The Passion Translation).

23

Failure, Go!

...You have anointed my head with oil; my cup overflows. Surely goodness and lovingkindness will follow me all the days of my life, and I will dwell in the house of the Lord forever (Psalm 23:5-6).

I WAS MEDITATING ON THIS SCRIPTURE ONE DAY WHEN THE LORD came to me in a vision and literally started pouring His presence over my entire body. A gold substance flowed over my head as I saw His giant hand holding a ladle over me. The liquid's warmth drenched my body, and like a sealed stamp from the Lord, I felt a crown being placed on my head. The gold substance dripped from my body, as I was completely drenched. This wasn't a small sprinkling baptism; this was a complete drenching of God's presence!

Then I heard God's voice audibly say, "I'm washing you and the Church right now of the enemy's most recent attacks. He's trying to make you feel like a failure. I just released you now from this lie and redressed your head with gold, honor, and royalty."

We all know it. The enemy comes to *"steal, kill, and destroy"* (John 10:10), but sometimes it is so hard to recognize it is him at work in our lives. He creeps in the back door like an unwanted guest in our house. He speaks lies over us and twists the truth of the Lord until we forget who we are in Christ. He takes up residence like a squatter when we agree with his lies. He sinks his talons into our hearts when others wound us, and we become bitter. He destroys relationships by getting in our thoughts and words toward each other, and he creates barriers. Like an undesirable construction worker, he helps us build up walls in our own heart, pulling us farther away from others, and farther away from the love of God. And yet, we sometimes allow it.

There's good news! *"Therefore, if anyone is in Christ, the new creation has come. The old has gone, the new is here!"* (2 Cor. 5:17 NIV). When Christ took His place on the cross and took upon Himself the sins of the world and said, "It is finished!" (John 19:30), the separation between humanity and God was no more. We are sons and daughters and heirs of Christ. He makes us new. He renews us with His love, grace, and mercy, again and again and again. Through the mercy of the cross, we are set free from the enemy's lies and attacks. God raises us up to the royal priesthood we are in Him.

As I was drenched that afternoon, I encourage you to immerse yourself in the truth today. You are not a failure. You are victorious in Him! And you are made *new.*

24

It's Your Inheritance

And Jesus cried out again with a loud voice, and yielded up His spirit. And behold, the veil of the temple was torn in two from top to bottom; and the earth shook and the rocks were split (Matthew 27:50-51).

IT'S SO EASY TO OVERLOOK IT. WE KNOW THE SCRIPTURES; WE'VE heard the story, but do we like to revisit what Jesus went through so we can have eternity with Him?

> *While they were eating, Jesus took some bread, and after a blessing, He broke it and gave it to the disciples, and said, "Take, eat; this is My body." And when He had taken a cup and given thanks, He gave it to them, saying, "Drink from it, all of you; for this is My blood of the covenant, which is poured out for the forgiveness of sins"* (Matthew 26:26-28).

Oh the sacrifice—little do we know.

Once God took me up into a vision of Golgotha. I walked up a hill where I looked up and saw my King Jesus there, crucified on the cross. It was horrific. What His body looked like, there are no words to describe it really. I heard the mighty veil tearing. It was so loud! When the veil tore, and He took His final breath, the amount of power and glory that came off that cross was so tremendous that it knocked me off my feet.

I heard the Lord say, "You can come back here whenever you like." Then I felt healing start happening in my throat. Previously that day, I had been sick with a horrible head cold. When I could feel healing beginning to happen, at first I laid hands on my throat and prayed, but then I heard I should actually lay hands on my nose and sinuses as well. As I did this, I felt all the congestion in my nose and infection in my throat completely come out. All the pressure in my ears also released a little.

Just one drop of His blood was enough to cover all the sins of the world and bring healing to us all. We so often forget about the healing in the blood. So today, plead the blood of Christ over yourself. It's your inheritance! Claim it! Claim your healing.

25

Linens

But Peter got up and ran to the tomb; stooping
and looking in, he saw the linen wrappings
only; and he went away to his home, marveling
at what had happened (Luke 24:12).

OFTEN WHEN WE THINK OF THE TOMB OF CHRIST AND HOW IT WAS found empty, we don't think about the linens Christ was wrapped in. What that tomb saw, nobody knows—we can only marvel! The power of death and life resurrected happened within its walls. The linens bore a body that was crushed, bruised, beaten, and destroyed for our sins, and then healed, whole, and resurrected! The most incredible transformation ever recorded happened within those linens in that tomb.

Once, Jesus took me to the tomb. I was having a vision, and I walked up to a dirt area, and there before my eyes was an empty tomb. I saw the old cloths there, folded. For some reason, I wanted to touch the linens, so I asked Him, "Can I, Lord?" I felt like I had permission, so I reached out, and the moment my hands touched the tips of the cloths, I felt the immense love of the Father come over me. I felt in that moment, so loved, so accepted, and so free!

I felt God's mercy in a deeper way, penetrate my being. Situations in my life that were weighing heavy on me, in that moment, each was completely lifted off. A new direction and shift happened in my life. I heard then the Lord's voice speak to me in a tender way, "Let down your hair, girl, and be free." Ways that I had allowed fear to enter my life and even how I made decisions, were gone now. It's funny how we can actually be operating out of fear under the surface, in even the way we formulate opinions or base decisions. Even that was gone. And I felt truly free!

There are times God has reminded me of that vision. He'll take me back, show me the linens again, and remind me. "Which side of the tomb are you living from?" He asked me one day. As He held up the linens, He looked me in the eyes in the way that penetrates to my core and asked, "Are you still living in chains, or are you living from the resurrected side of the cross?"

That question, to this day, has stopped me in my tracks many times. Am I truly living in total freedom? It's made me want more! Any parent's deepest desire is to see their child walk in full confidence and freedom in who Christ made the child to be. I wonder sometimes, if God doesn't look down from Heaven, from His throne, and as He sees one of us going through struggles, with tender love in His eyes, He longs for us to get it. To know, taste, believe, and walk in our full freedom. To walk from the resurrected side of the cross. The linens lay empty.

26

Declaration and War Room

"I want to take you somewhere," I heard the Lord say one day. I had been sitting in my living room, listening to some worship music when I heard His voice. Immediately, I was up in a room of Heaven.

I've been to many different rooms of Heaven; each one encompassing a lesson for me, each one containing its own atmosphere—some being full of joy, some being full of the fear and reverence of the Lord. Today, I went to the declaration and war room. This isn't the name the Lord calls it, it's just what I've personally decided to call the room.

The atmosphere was exciting. The energy was high, as so much was going on. As I walked into the room, the first thing I noticed was Jesus in the very center. He seemed to be orchestrating the entire room. Angels bustled to and fro in the room; they were huge and majestic. Some wore armor and carried weapons. I was taken aback a little by their size and magnitude. They were dressed and ready to go into a war. Some of them blew horns at specific times while I was in this room, and they pointed the horn in a specific direction as they released its sound. I was sure they were releasing the presence of the King over a certain region of the world. The sound of the horns would release breakthrough. No matter what the angels did, though, they kept their eyes on the King in the center of the room. They were taking their cues from Him.

Next, I was drawn to and intrigued by the enormous amount of people in the room. They were dressed in white robes and carried a peace about them. Their mannerisms were a bit alarming to me at first. The peace, joy, and honest love they carried felt amazing—and showed me my own lack. Although they carried such peace, they weren't there to make peace; they were there to make war! Prayers, intercession, and declarations were made loudly throughout the room. Not one by one, but rather all at once. It sounded like a war cry. It sounded like thunder shattering the air.

That's when I decided I wanted to join in! I started crying out to God for healing from my generational lineage from certain things. I declared the breaking off of old generational curses and patterns. Like a fork in the road, I declared renewal for my kids and future grand-kids. I cried out for the presence of the King to be released over the earth. I cried out with hunger for Jesus to increase over the earth. I shouted out prayers for apostolic wisdom and leadership to rise up over the entire world. Last, I shouted praise for the King I love, who was seated there in the middle of it all.

I believe in the power of prayer and intercession with all my heart. I believe that there are things being released in the spiritual realm, whether I see them or not, when I partner with God and pray and declare what's on His heart.

First John 5:14-15 says, *"This is the confidence which we have before Him, that, if we ask anything according to His will, He hears us. And if we know that He hears us in whatever we ask, we know that we have the requests which we have asked from Him."* So, whether or not I can see the fruit or the answers to my prayers now, I know with confidence that a seed is planted when I pray.

Would you join with Him today? Whether or not you can see the declaration and war room, would you join the King today and make intercession? Would you pray like you really believe there is power in your prayers?

27

Ouch—But You're Still Good

We all desire to live pain free. It was never the Father's desire for us to feel and experience pain, disease, and sickness. Adam and Eve had it made! They could eat from all but one tree. They were totally provided for, had authority in The Garden to rule over everything, and could dwell with God Himself at any time. Can you imagine what that would be like? (See Gen. 2.)

Then, through the temptation of the serpent, the Fall of humankind happened. Although our way to reach the Father has been redeemed by the glorious cross, we were driven out of Eden. Sickness and pain is part of this world now. Sometimes I catch myself thinking, *Man, you two screwed it up for us big time!*

I know that God is the God who heals. No matter how many times I pray for healing, and some get healed and some don't, I always keep praying. I never understand why some get their healing and others don't, but I'm not God.

I was having one of those days—you know those days—you wake up and just want to roll over and go back to sleep in the comfort of your bed, then face the reality of the day later. It was one of those days. I woke up and felt like I had a full-blown sinus infection. I had been taking care of my kids and husband who all week had been down with bad colds. Finally, it was my turn. I thought that by some glorious miracle I had cheated this round of sickness in our house, but nope. Reality set in after a week of pushing myself beyond my limits, and my body was telling me it was time to put on the brakes.

"Why, God, oh why am I sick?" I prayed. I heard nothing in response. So I started to pray, asking the Lord to take the sickness from me. I started claiming Scripture, "By Your stripes I've been healed!" (see Isa. 53:5). "I declare healing now over my entire body, that infection must leave my body. In Jesus' name, GO!" I said out loud.

And still no response. As I lay there, miserable, with my head pounding, finally I asked the right question, "Where are You in this, God?" Then I heard His voice, "The reason you are healing right now so quickly is by My power. There is pain, but I am with you through it all. The Lion of Judah walks with you. It's not the ability to avoid pain, but to conquer and remain victorious, and not lose your focus on Me through it all."

Ouch. Although not exactly what I wanted to hear in that moment, it was still a statement so full of love. Although we can't always see that God is moving, Jesus is always interceding on our behalf. He is good, even when we can't understand. Trust is knowing that God is still good, no matter the outcome or suffering or amount of waiting involved.

> Yet, with respect to the promise of God, he did not waver in unbelief, he did not waver in unbelief but grew strong in faith, giving glory to God, and being fully assured that what God had promised, He was able also to perform (Romans 4:20).

28

Four Wisdoms

ONE DAY I WAS ASKED BY A FRIEND FOR ADVICE. AFTER I PRAYED FOR a while and sought out the Lord, I felt like I had some wisdom to share with this friend. As we talked on the phone, no matter how I phrased what I had heard in love, it was not received well. Have you ever had that experience? It's like no matter what's spoken through that phone line, the receiving end is broken and the message isn't heard accurately.

After the phone conversation, I was frustrated and honestly a little offended. I know what to do with offense every time—I go to Him with it. "God, I'm offended and I know it's not right. Please heal my heart. Forgive me for getting frustrated and offended too quickly. I need Your perspective," I prayed.

Instantly, I saw in a vision two large hands. They were closed as fists at first, and then I saw them open. As they opened, a perfume smell was released from them and filled my nostrils. It was a smell that projected the feeling of peace in the air.

Then I heard Jesus say these four phases: "Pursue Kingdom. Pursue Gospel. Pursue Trust. Pursue Faith." These four wisdoms from the Lord are foundational for me. During various seasons, the Lord will highlight one of these or maybe even a few that I need to refocus on and grow in a little more. That day with my friend, I needed to refocus on all of them.

Pursue Kingdom. Hmmm…the Bible says a lot about Kingdom values. The Beatitudes sermon, in Matthew chapter 5, is so rich: *"Blessed are the poor in spirit, for theirs is the kingdom of heaven. Blessed are the peacemakers, for they shall be called children of God"* (Matt. 5:3,9 NIV). I read these verses and instantly felt convicted to pray a prayer, "Lord, let me be a person of peace. I pray and declare peace into my relationship with my friend. Show me how to go low, how to humble myself, and how to love more."

Pursue Gospel. Often the Scripture used for pursuing the Gospel is, "Heal the sick, raise the dead, cleanse the lepers, cast out demons…" (Matt. 10:8), but what follows this verse is key: "Whoever does not receive you, nor heed your words, as you go out of that house or that city, shake the dust off your feet" (Matt. 10:14). I read that verse that day, and knew what God was speaking to me—let no offense lay on your heart. I had done everything I knew to do to approach the person in love; I waited to hear from the Lord what to say, I tried to explain myself in love; I honored the person as I spoke, and yet it was still not received well. So it was time to just simply shake it off. Letting go and not holding on to offense is a key for every person to stay out of the enemy's path. Easier said than done sometimes, but still necessary!

Pursue Trust and Pursue Faith. When I heard these two phrases, I instantly began to pray, "God, I trust You with this relationship. I hand it over to You; it's Yours. Ultimately, though, no matter the outcome, I trust You. I will have faith that You are good no matter the outcome. God, I have faith that if You desire me to have this person in my life and have this friendship, then You will do something surprising and repair it. Mend what's been broken if it's Your will. Thank You, Lord."

After I prayed through these four wisdoms God had given me, I thought back to those hands opening that I had seen. I ended up praying this prayer, one I have used many times since, "God, I release them into Your hands, to pursue Your heart, Your Kingdom, and Your love. Amen."

Peace crashed in.

29

Shower of Heaven

How priceless is your unfailing love, O God! People take refuge in the shadow of your wings. They feast on the abundance of your house; you give them drink from your river of delights. For with you is the fountain of life; in your light we see light (Psalm 36:7-9 NIV).

CAN YOU FEEL GOD? CAN YOU REALLY FEEL HIM RIGHT NOW, RIGHT where you are, right next to you? Some days it's not enough just to *know* of His love and nature, but we have to *feel* it. We need a refreshing outpouring of His Spirit in our lives.

Like this Scripture passage in Psalm 36 we need to drink our fill of Him. There are many ways to get full of God. Reading the Word is always my starting place when I need to hear from Him. The Word is so rich and life-giving. Praying to Him and also worship connects me intimately to the Father.

But there are moments when God encounters me in a different way—through visions, experiences, and moments of feeling His presence in a real, tangible way. He shows up and surprises me anew.

I was sitting in my living room one day praying, and I felt water dripping down my back. It was so real, that I literally looked up to investigate where my ceiling might be leaking. As I looked up, I realized I was not in my living room anymore. I could see straight upward into Heaven. Angels were moving all about, happily carrying about their assignments. Even the air felt different. It was crisp and fresh, like being outdoors on a warm fresh morning—very different from inside my house.

I looked forward and briefly saw the Father God walk toward me. He told me to "Walk forward." I did so, with my arms open. When I moved forward, I walked right into what seemed like an open shower. There was a shower pouring straight down from Heaven on me. As the water rushed down my back, for I was now completely drenched, I could feel the heavy presence of the Lord all over me. I felt almost "zingy," the best way I can think to describe it. His presence gave me energy, joy, peace, and excitement—all mixed into that shower. A rush of energy surged through my body. From head to toe, I could feel Him.

Then I heard, "You will feel differently after this. I'm giving you a fresh sensitivity to Me. Stay in this shower of my presence throughout the day."

Then, just like that, I was back in my living room. I could still tangibly feel the presence of the King on me, and His weighty presence also felt very weighty in my home. Throughout the day at certain times, God would take me back there, for a second or third dousing of that heavenly shower.

Looking back on this experience, I was in a place that day where I really needed a fresh encounter with Him. I love how John writes about the river of God in Revelation, *"Then he showed me a river of the water of life, clear as crystal, coming from the throne of God and of the Lamb"* (Rev. 22:1). We humans consist mostly of water, about 60 to 70 percent, actually. The average person can live only three days without water. Without water, we perish. Do you see the connection? Without God, we perish. Isn't it amazing that as He was creating the heavens and the earth, God made a river flowing from His very throne, knowing that humans cannot survive without water. The metaphor can't be overlooked! We cannot survive without Him.

So today, you may be reading this and thinking, *YES! Sign me up! I need a fresh encounter!* I pray for you, "May the Lord come now and touch you. May you experience His presence in a deeper and richer way. I pray you also experience that heavenly shower. Let the waters that flow from His throne come now and wash away the worries and harshness of the day, and replenish your body, soul, and spirit.

He's with you now. Can you feel Him?

Rest in the Process

IT HAD ALREADY BEEN MANY YEARS SINCE I FIRST HEARD A PROMISE of God over my life. You see, it had always been in my heart to write a book. I wrote my first book when I was just a little girl, talking all about how I loved my parents, and pet bunny, dancing ballet, and life. I was really serious about getting it published! My parents kept it, just to support me at the time, and because it's one of those memories parents love to keep.

I had long forgotten that dream God put inside me. It was buried way down deep among other pursued dreams in my life. But God had not forgotten. It was buried down so deep that when God asked me to write a book one day, I didn't even remember about that first book—until I came across it at my parents' house.

So obediently, I began to write. I wrote the book God laid on my heart. But the process of getting published as a first-time author is pretty tough and daunting. So with no doors opening for me, and publishing houses and opportunities feeling closed and shut down, I did my best to muster up my faith and still believe.

Are you still believing for something today?

I asked God one day why I was still writing, with no promise in sight. What was I to do with my book once I completed it, when there were no open doors for publication?

And then I heard His response, "Find rest in Me. Trust me in the movement when you can't see. You are good enough. Get your focus on Me and Me alone. Don't look at the process, just look at me. I am your King and I open the doors."

Then I saw steps leading up to Heaven. They were lit up with golden light and were very steep. Up and up I climbed until I reached the top. There I found absolute stillness. The stillness made me feel a little uneasy at first. "Do you trust Me?" I heard the same voice ask. "Do you really trust Me? You would believe in Me, then believe in yourself."

A hard conversation with God, but a good reality check. Trust is being able to rest in the process. To set my focus on something other than that unfulfilled promise; to focus on God and know that He is bigger. To relinquish my own control and give it over to God. To believe when there is nothing to show for it—that's faith! And to have the courage to believe in myself and the promise of God in the drought.

> *...But Elijah went up to the top of Carmel; and he crouched down on the earth and put his face between his knees. He said to his servant, "Go up now, look toward the sea." So he went up and looked and said, "There is nothing." And he said, "Go back" seven times. It came about at the seventh time, that he said, "Behold a cloud as small as a man's hand is coming up from the sea." ...In a little while the sky grew black with clouds and wind, and there was a heavy shower...* (1 Kings 18:42-45).

31

As Close as You Want

"Listen! My Beloved! Behold, he is coming,
climbing on the mountains, leaping on the hills!
...A voice! My beloved was knocking... Let his
left hand be under my head and his right hand
embrace me" (Song of Solomon 2:8, 5:2, 2:6).

EVERY SO OFTEN WE HAVE MOMENTS AS BELIEVERS IN CHRIST WHEN we feel Him really close to us. It's like the veil between Heaven and earth is pulled back just a little thinner, and He makes His appearance. God is always in pursuit of us, whether we recognize it or not. He is a gentle Father, though, and always gives us the choice of whether to accept His invitation to come a little closer, to embrace Him a little deeper, and pursue Him a little more.

One day, I had one of those close encounters with God. Out of my desperation to get closer to Him, and to feel Him in the middle of my day, the Lion of Judah came to me. Just like that, He was standing in my living room. His very presence caused me to hit the ground in reverence.

"Come closer. Come as close as you want," I heard Him say. With my head bowed down, a little afraid to look up into His eyes, I approached the Lion. Gathering up my courage, I looked quickly up into His face and laughed at seeing the Lion of Judah smiling back at me. His eyes were so full of love, so full of light. They looked so kind and gentle.

So I ran up to Him and curled up next to His hair. I ran my fingers through His mane, and felt the warmth of God. He let me sit there next to Him as long as I wanted. I wanted this moment to last forever. Never had I felt so loved, so safe, so free to be myself as in this moment, sitting next to the giant Lion.

I asked Him then to restore my joy. I had taken on stress over the week and was carrying it around like a bad odor. (Now there's a nice word picture!) "Stress is not my portion," I heard myself say out loud. "I want the ever-flowing joy of the Lord. The joy of the Lord is my strength."

The Lion looked at me and smiled, and nodded in agreement. Turning, He brushed by me, and I felt electricity shoot through my body, or warmth and presence, mixed with joy. That literally is the best way I can describe it! Fatigue and stress felt brushed off me, and left on me was His joy and presence.

And then just like that, the Lion of Judah was gone.

He'll come as close as you want. As close as you're desperate for. As hungry as you are. He's knocking at the door, just waiting for you. Won't you invite Him in.

32

His Friend

I LOVE READING PEOPLE'S PERSONAL STORIES! I LOVE TO SHARE MY stories about the fun journeys God has taken me on. Jesus taught in stories and so I think sharing stories is the best way to relate to people, and also to teach.

God knows me well, and He knows how I am very visual. I was one of those kids who learned best if I could see it. Show me the concept in a picture first, and then I could learn it and teach it back.

Many times, God will show me a vision of my relationship with Him, and correct me through it. There are times when He'll say, "Come here, Ana. I want to show you something," and then He'll take me up in a vision.

I've seen myself sitting way far away from the Father in a great big room. I try and stand up and run toward Him, but it's like my feet are cemented to the ground, and no matter how many times I try, I can't shorten the distance between myself and Him.

God has shown me this picture to reveal sin in my heart that needs to get cleaned out and how it puts distance in our relationship. Other times He has used it to teach me the falsehood that I am believing, that I am far from Him, when in reality I am not.

Today, I walked hand in hand with Jesus. We walked along the shoreline at a beach and talked heart to heart. I told Him how much I loved Him, and how much I had recently missed having time with Him. I told Him my specific prayer requests and concerns for my family. Gently, He listened. Very rarely did He give me advice, but rather listened with a loving heart. I asked Him questions, some of which He answered, others He left unanswered. He asked me deep questions to ponder: Where was I going? What was His heart for a situation? What was I still wrestling with in fear? Who could I love for Him today?

Our time together on that shoreline was too short, as is every encounter I have with Jesus. When I am in that moment, nothing else matters. I just want to stay with Him forever in that place. He really is that good. He really does love that much.

I think of Michelangelo's painting "The Creation of Adam," where God's hand is outstretched toward man's. To think that we can really walk hand in hand with Jesus is beyond my comprehension. That the God who is omnipotent would want to hold my hand and have relationship with me, and call me His friend, is truly amazing.

Do you see yourself as His friend?

How blessed is the one whom You choose and bring near to You to dwell in Your courts. We will be satisfied with the goodness of Your house, Your holy temple (Psalm 65:4).

33

A Stamp from God

ALWAYS THE ENEMY RISES UP AGAINST US TO TRY TO STEAL, ROB, AND destroy our hope and security in Christ. I was having one of those weeks, or actually one of those months. I had taken on a new form of leadership at the church's healing rooms. Fresh ideas were coming to me, but change isn't always an easy course to implement to a system that had been the same way for over fourteen years. I knew that change wouldn't be easy.

I prayed about it, "God, You've asked me to do this. I know You've placed me here to be instrumental in the move of the healing rooms, and help build it up. I know You want some changes, but not everyone likes change. What am I supposed to do?"

As soon as that last phrase came out of my lips to God, I instantly knew and said out loud, "Ah ha! The enemy is at work here to try and steal my joy and excitement to be in a leadership role regarding the healing rooms. I must be doing something right!"

I was pondering over all this, sitting in the sanctuary of the church. It was during soaking time when our healing teams all worship in the presence of the Lord, before we open the healing rooms for the public to come and receive prayer. I opened my eyes, looked up, and saw a giant angel standing right in front of my face. It truly did scare me at first because of its enormity and close proximity to my body. Smiling, the angel lifted its hand that was carrying what looked like a large rubber stamp. *Boom,* it stamped my forehead! "The mark of leadership and authority," it said. Then the Lord said, "Let no one stop what I have set in place." *Well, that was a new experience! Thank You, Jesus,* I thought to myself.

You know what I have learned from that experience with God? The Lord's stamp is all I need. As long as I'm walking in the Lord's will and purpose, then it's not my job to fret or worry. Now, that doesn't mean I can't receive wisdom from others or lose my ability to maintain a teachable spirit. Often though, the enemy uses old tactics. He tries to rob my peace and confidence. He tries to make me waver and wonder if I truly heard the Lord correctly. Trust in the Lord your God with all your heart, spirit, and soul, right? Not in people or the enemy.

So what is the mark of the Lord over your life? May the Lord reveal to you what He is calling you to do for this season. May you feel the mark of approval and acceptance of the Lord upon you, and never waver in your confidence in Him.

> *Then David said to his son Solomon, "Be strong and courageous, and act; do not fear nor be dismayed, for the Lord God, my God, is with you. He will not fail you nor forsake you until all the work for the service of the house of the Lord is finished"* (1 Chronicles 28:20).

34

Rise Up, Resist, and Declare

Do you want to be on the victorious side? Are you tired of being on the defense and want to live on the offense with Christ? Are you tired of feeling beaten up by the enemy?

I went through a really tough season with my son when he was first born. He had tummy problems, and test after test revealed nothing, absolutely nothing! Frustrated after being advised to put my new baby through one more test, and try one more thing, I turned to God.

"God, where are You in all this? You are my Healer. You created and knit together my son in my womb. You know what is going on with Him, Lord. Please come help me, Lord. I'm tired and worn out by all these doctors' questions and tests. I don't want to sit by and watch my baby crying as they poke him one more time. I just want him whole and happy and well."

Then I heard the Lord's voice in response, "Rise up, Ana. Declare what you want to see. There is power in your words. Pray against a spirit of discouragement that you are up against. Resist the enemy's arrows. It's time to battle, and I will help you."

Then I saw an image of a white war horse running through deep waters, and I sensed healing was at hand. So I began to declare like I believed that my declarations had the power of God behind them.

"I declare in Jesus' name that my son's stomach will be healed now and he will be able to handle all foods. I declare that Ellis (my son) would start sleeping peacefully and that there would be no weapon formed against him, in the name of Jesus. I declare the truth, that God will not give me more than I can handle, and that I am a good mother! Ellis and I will enjoy life together as mother and son, and not live in stress anymore. I declare joy in this household and peace. And I declare that I will carry a spirit of peace even in the unrest. God is my strength and He is mighty to save. So I declare now that God is saving my family from all weapons of the enemy, and they must go now. I plead the blood of Christ over my entire family! AMEN!"

You know what, my son was healed. Just like that, his stomach began to heal on its own. He stopped having so many problems, and I began to feel the peace and joy of the Lord back in our household.

Do you know today how powerful you are in Christ? The enemy is actually scared of believers in Jesus who know and walk in the authority of Christ. So how should that change your own prayers and declarations? When we make agreements with Heaven and speak out those words of God over ourselves, we shift the atmosphere. We stand in the revelation and truth that "all authority has been given to me by the Father."

Washing Off Defeat

*In my distress I called upon the Lord, and
cried to my God for help; He heard my voice
out of His temple, and my cry for help before
Him came into His ears* (Psalm 18:6).

It's good to know God hears our cries and that He's big enough to take them! No matter what situation you find yourself in today, He cares. I reassure you, *He cares!* It's hard to feel it when you're in turmoil or the swirl of pain or hardship, but He cares.

Today the Lord brought me back to an old entry in a journal.

I looked down, and there I saw my feet covered in dirt. Why are they so dirty? I thought. Why am I covered in dirt? "Come back to me. Lay it at my feet. Breakthrough is close, so hang in there. Wash off defeat. Brush it off just like shaking off this dirt off your feet. I am near," I heard Him say.

Today, I am declaring for myself and for you, dear reader, that truly there's no mountain too great that He cannot move! We must stand in faith and not waiver. Let's brush defeat off ourselves right now, and claim that victory is at hand. Defeat is exactly what the enemy wants to coat us with. Like a heavy coat of dust wrapped around our shoulders, it tries to drown us out. But, no more, in Jesus' name! Let's claim our victory, whether we feel it or not, and wash off defeat.

36

Esther Anointing

Suddenly, I found myself walking into the great throne room. I instantly felt like I didn't belong there. Everything in me wanted to run back out, but curiosity glued my feet like cement to the ground. Insecurity hit me at every level as I saw at a glance the mighty throne and Him upon it. I hit the floor in reverence and could barely will myself to lift my eyes and look at the bottom of His robe draped on the floor around the front of the throne. There were thousands of people in the room, all worshiping. I could see and sense angelic presence everywhere. The room was so alive with joyful expectation and adoration of the One who sat on the throne.

I felt my face get hot to the touch, as I could feel His glance rest upon me. "Ana," I heard God say, "You must see yourself as a queen when you enter here, not as a beggar." At that, I lifted my eyes just in time to catch Him rise from the mighty throne and extend a scepter toward me. "Queen Esther anointing," I heard Holy Spirit whisper.

Just like that, the vision was over, and I was back in my home with my Bible still open where I had been reading before. Quickly I flipped the pages to Esther's story, and my eyes rested on Esther chapter 5.

Now it came about on the third day that Esther put on her royal robes and stood in the inner court of the king's palace in front of the king's rooms, and the king was sitting on his royal throne in the throne room opposite the entrance to the palace. When the king saw Esther the queen standing in the court, she obtained favor in his sight and the king extended to Esther the golden scepter which was in his hand. So Esther came near and touched the top of the scepter (Esther 5:1-2).

Ever since that encounter with the throne room and my interaction with God, God has healed how I view myself and how I personally enter into His presence. Like a beggar, before I saw myself through a lens of unworthiness and that getting close to God was for others, not me. I'd seen others go before me and have close encounters with the Father Himself, but was that truly for me? Would God really want me to draw near to Him? Like a hidden valley, my own insecurity caused a gap between God and myself.

In an instant He pulled back the layers that needed to come off— my beggar's clothes. He rewrapped me in royal robes and spoke over me my value to Him. He taught me to never crawl again in front of Him, believing the lie that He doesn't want me to draw near to Him. He taught me to *stand,* just as Esther stood in His inner courts, in His very presence.

Dignity is not about being proud, but rather knowing who you are in His eyes. He values you and sees you as worthy of His love. But the true and vital question is, "Do you?"

37

Canopy Influence

THERE I SAW A GIANT TREE. THE TREE LOOKED SIMILAR TO THE BAObab trees that my husband and I saw when we lived briefly in Mozambique, Africa. From the ground looking upward, the trunk looked enormous, thick, and abnormally straight. Under the trunk I sat, and looked straight upward at the branches above. The branches shot out like an umbrella to form a green canopy that blocked my view from seeing beyond this tree.

Hmmm, what's the Lord up to? I thought to myself. Just then, He took me to the top of the tree. I found myself sitting on the very top branch quite high up.

"Lord, what am I doing here?" I asked Him. "You know I don't like heights! Why are we here? I want to get down."

"I want you to change your position. It's time for you to look up and get wisdom from above. Change your perspective and focus. Come close to Me. Then you can have influence. But you must remain here. Canopy influence."

> *Acquire wisdom! Acquire understanding! Do not forget nor turn away from the words of my mouth. Do not forsake her, and she will guard you; love her,*

and she will watch over you. The beginning of wisdom is: acquire wisdom; and with all your acquiring, get understanding. Prize her, and she will exalt you; she will honor you if you embrace her (Proverbs 4:5-8).

It's amazing how perspective can give us a completely different outcome on the way we treat or react to something in life. As we draw closer to Him today, let's ask Him for His perspective. What we draw near to influences us, whether good or bad. We begin to act and think like the things that we allow to be close to us. All that we open ourselves up to—whether certain ways of thinking, what we see or invite into our lives, friendships, even conversations—influence us whether we realize it or not.

As we draw near to Him and set our eyes on the Author and Perfecter of faith, we begin to smell like Him; we begin to exhibit His nature and character, and we see from a heavenly perspective.

So draw near to Him, remain close to Him, and receive heavenly perspective—not only for yourself, but also for the people you might influence.

38

Pool of Joy

We walked hand in hand through His Garden. Usually, in previous times Jesus would allow me to explore His Garden, but this time I could tell He had an agenda. This time He held my hand, but was leading me toward a destination. My heart felt excited! I thought, *He's leading me to show me something new!*

"Yes, I am, Ana," Jesus said as He looked back at me. Still, to this day it surprises me when God responds to my thoughts out loud. In my head, I know God knows everything, but still it does surprise me when He responds.

We walked through The Garden, down long paths lined with many vibrantly colored flowers, until finally we came upon a clearing. There I saw many pools with fountains of water springing up from the pools. He led me to look into the pools, and there I saw that the color of the water was not just one color, but many swirling colors. The water looked alive and dancing with excitement at His presence being near.

Jesus led me to one specific pool. "Drink from this," He said, and motioned for me to drink. I cupped my hands and slurped up the water. It tasted sweet, unlike anything I ever drank. I felt immediately refreshed and energized.

"This is a pool of joy. You need to come and get refreshed. I am pulling you through this season. Rely on Me. I will help you," Jesus said.

> *That vision is one I keep in my treasure box of encounters with Jesus. When I am going through a hard season and feeling exhausted, afraid, or just dried up, I remind God of when He took me to that pool. I remind Him of His promise to me that "I can do all things through him who strengthens me" (Philippians 4:13).*

It's always interesting to me that in that encounter Jesus didn't say, "I'm removing you from this circumstance" or "I've fought this battle for you, and the battle is won. The battle's over," but rather He said, "I am pulling you through."

Today, whatever life is throwing at you, know that God is pulling you through. May you be refreshed by Him. May your joy be restored supernaturally. And may you find the strength you didn't know you had to keep going and never give up. You're not a quitter! You are a victorious one!

> *He changes a wilderness into a pool of water and a dry land into springs of water (Psalm 107:35).*

39

Pierce the Clouds

THE BEGINNING OF THE GOSPEL OF JESUS CHRIST, THE SON OF GOD. As it is written in Isaiah the prophet: "Behold, I send My messenger ahead of You, who will prepare Your way; the voice of one crying in the wilderness, 'Make ready the way of the Lord, make His paths straight."

John the Baptist appeared in the wilderness preaching a baptism of repentance for the forgiveness of sins. And all the country of Judea was going out to him, and all the people of Jerusalem; and they were being baptized by him in the Jordan River, confessing their sins. John was clothed with camel's hair and wore a leather belt around his waist, and his diet was locust and wild honey. And he was preaching, and saying, "After me One is coming who is mightier than I, and I am not fit to stoop down and untie the thong of His sandals. I baptized you with water; but He will baptize you with the Holy Spirit" (Mark 1:1-8).

Do you have a calling or urge in your heart to live the abnormal lifestyle for Jesus? I know I do! I am constantly praying a prayer that goes like this: "God, get me out of my box! Stretch my faith muscles, because I want to run after You. I pray that You would give me no more than I can handle, but more than I think I can handle, so that I can grow! Don't let me stay comfortable!"

Once God gave me a vision. After a time of prayer, He showed me a picture of myself carrying a large spear. I was in a stormy place, that was heavy and full with rain clouds. The heaviness of the load those rain clouds were carrying almost felt oppressive.

"Pierce the clouds," I heard Him say. So immediately, I started jumping up and piercing the clouds with my tall spear. I saw spurts of light rays bursting from the clouds and showering down on the earth below. They were so strong it seemed like I was looking into laser beams. I could see healing dripping from the light, and the words "HOPE RENEWED." His presence was pouring down upon the earth.

I love John the Baptist. He wasn't someone who could be placed in the religious box of that time period. The guy wore camel's hair, and ate bugs and honey! Pretty out of the ordinary. I can only wonder what the Pharisees of that time thought of John when they saw Him. "How sacrilegious!" they might have said among themselves.

There are many things that separate John from others, but one thing that sticks out is that John wasn't succumbed by fear. He was free. He was so sure of God and His identity in Him, that God could use him in a mighty way! He prophesied the coming of the King, without excuse, without apology, without watering down his message.

God is raising up mighty lovers of Him who are willing to pierce through the clouds to bring His presence. Will you allow yourself to get uncomfortable? Do you want your faith muscles stretched? Dare to ask Him for it today.

40

Stop. Find Me

"Be quiet. Take a moment, and find Me here. Find Me in the midst of your busy schedule. Stop what you are doing; surrender your schedule and find Me," I heard His gentle whisper say to me this morning.

Then I saw a picture of a gentle brook. I stood by the shore and dipped my feet into the cool, rushing water that bubbled on over my feet.

"OK, God. But what about..." The list of things I had on my plans for the day seemed endless. It consumed every thought and every moment with God this morning. I even intentionally tried to quiet my mind. *OK,* I thought, *I'm not going to think about that list of groceries I need to make or that project I want to do with the kids today or the meeting I have to prepare for this afternoon.*

But then, there they would be. The list of tasks returning to the front of my mind. My thoughts and time were consumed.

Do you ever find yourself in my situation? Ever so busy that you can't even be quiet with God? It's like we are so used to hustling about through life, that being silent and still feels like a chore. It's even uncomfortable.

"But God, what about…?!" becomes our regular thoughts and conversations with Him, whether we realize it or not. Like a worker bee on a sunny day, we buzz about from task to task, seeking to find peace and utmost happiness once everything gets accomplished—which it never does.

"Stop. Find Me," He whispers to me again.

And, finally I got still. I let it all go, and I got still with God. It took a while, but finally I got there.

"I love you," He smiled and said. Just one quick glance, but I saw Jesus' smile. The words felt like medicine to my soul.

A perfect way to start the day.

> *You will seek Me and find Me when you search for Me with all your heart* (Jeremiah 29:13).

41

Healing Waters

*...and he led me through the water, water reaching
the ankles. Again he measured a thousand and led me
through the water, water reaching the knees. Again
he measured a thousand and led me through the
water, water reaching the loins. Again he measured
a thousand; and it was a river that I could not ford,
for the water had risen, enough water to swim in,
a river that could not be forded* (Ezekiel 47:3-5).

*It will come about that every living creature
which swarms in every place where the
river goes, will live...* (Ezekiel 47:9).

ONE DAY, I ACTUALLY EXPERIENCED THIS VERSE WITH THE LORD. I
woke up immensely sick with a horrible head cold. The pressure in my
face and sinuses was too much to bear. I had tried every natural remedy I knew to ward off the sickness, but the pressure would not cease.

"God, help!" I cried out to Him. "I'm so sick, and I have so much
pain. Won't You please come relieve it? Please heal me! Please come
take it away!"

Have you ever cried out to God like that? Can you relate right now? It's not a faith-filled prayer at all, but more one out of desperation. Are you desperate today for Him to come and break into your situation?

Finishing my prayer, I closed my Bible. It was pointless for me to try and even read it. The pain and pressure behind my sinuses were too strong to even keep my eyes open. I laid down and shut my eyes.

"I need You, God. Please help me," I prayed.

Just then, I saw myself with Jesus. He smiled at me, took my hand, and led me to the edge of a river. I looked at the water, which was not calm. "Lord, couldn't You have led me to a gentle stream? I'm pretty sick right now!" I laughed and asked Him.

He laughed back at me, and with a gleam of joy in His eyes, He responded, "Not today. Today this is the water I've chosen for you."

He led me into the river until I was knee-deep in it. I was grateful that this time He walked with me and helped me brace the current in my weakness.

"That's far enough," He instructed me. "Place the sword I have given you in the water."

I hadn't even realized that my sword was there with us. I grabbed it and placed it in the water. As I sunk it as far as I could into the deep sand below, I felt strength suddenly pulsating through my being; strength to stand in the midst of the strong current.

"I declare right now, by His stripes I have been healed. It says in Your Word, Lord, that coming from Your throne there is a river of life that carries healing to the nations (Rev. 22), so I declare right now that I have been healed and this sickness must go now, in Jesus' name!" I yelled.

And then I was back on my couch lying down. The vision was over, but the impact was lasting. The pain and pressure in my head was totally gone. My body had been healed.

Let Him lead you out into His healing presence today. Let Him instruct you how to use your sword of the Spirit to war against the enemy's attacks. Let Him carry you through the waters. Hand in hand, He assists us all. Let Him help you brace the current and become victorious. He is for you, not against you.

42

Living Room Chats

"Come as close as you want. Come just as you are." I woke up one morning hearing this song being sung over me.

"Share with Me what's on your heart today. Don't hold back," I heard then the Father gently say to me.

Instantly, I was in a living room setting. I could see the warmth of a fire and hear it crack and sizzle the wet logs. I was having a vision of being in a living room with the Father. I found myself sitting on a comfy couch, by the warmth of a fire. I saw the Father sitting beside me. I couldn't look directly at Him, but I recognized it was His presence there beside me.

"It's OK. You can share with Me," the voice reassured me.

Taking a moment, I looked in the fire, trying to gather my thoughts and words. Yesterday had been overwhelming, really. I was confronted with new fear that I never knew I had. A situation I found myself in uncovered new pressures, new fears, and new insecurities deep from within me.

"I feel like I'm failing, Lord," I said apologetically to Him. "I feel all this pressure on me with all the different roles I balance on a daily basis, and I feel like I just can't keep up. There's this big event coming up, God, that I have to find time to prepare for. What if You don't come through Lord?"

Immediately, I felt silly for making that last statement. Of course the Lord will always come through for me; I knew it in my heart, but fear was overriding. Life was swirling at a fast pace for my husband and me. With two babies at home, a nonprofit, a full-time ministry, healing rooms to manage, and my husband's full-time business, the fact that I was feeling a little overwhelmed at that moment was completely rational. Or was it?

"Give your burdens to Me," He said, smiling. "Hand them over. I've got them. I will help you. Let's do this together."

Immediately I felt the relief that I so needed that evening. It's not that Jesus took away my responsibilities, but He took the pressure away for me to manage them all by myself. I was doing things in my own strength instead of relying on Him. Knowing that we could handle things together made all the difference. It changed my outlook. As I started preparing for the big event I had coming up, the moment I started to feel overwhelmed, I went to God and asked Him for help. Every time He showed up.

Do not strive in your own efforts today. Turn to Him.

Cast your burden upon the Lord and He will sustain you; He will never allow the righteous to be shaken (Psalm 55:22).

43

R-I-S-K

Therefore that disciple whom Jesus loved said to Peter, "It is the Lord." So when Simon Peter heard that it was the Lord, he put his outer garment on (for he was stripped for work), and threw himself into the sea. But the other disciples came in the little boat, for they were not far from the land, but about one hundred yards away, dragging the net full of fish. So when they got out on the land, they saw a charcoal fire already laid and fish placed on it, and bread. Jesus said to them, "Bring some of the fish which you have now caught. Simon Peter went up and drew the net to the land, full of large fish, a hundred and fifty-three; and although there were so many, the net was not torn (John 21:7-11).

YOU GOT TO LOVE PETER'S ZEAL! THEY ARE ONLY 100 YARDS AWAY from the shoreline. (A small distance for a boat, but a nice long distance for a swimmer.) And yet, Peter jumps instantly out of the boat and swims out to meet Jesus. I read this story and think, *Why? Why did he swim when it was completely unnecessary? Was he trying to prove something? What was his motivation?*

97

Jesus was his motivation. He couldn't wait to meet the One he loved. Simon Peter is known to be an extreme character in the Bible, and for that I love him! He is pretty impulsive and emotional. From jumping out of the boat, like this Scripture states, to swim out to Jesus, to cutting off the ear of the Centurion's servant, Peter makes some rash decisions.

But here's what I think. There is something about the combination of zeal and passion mixed with faith to jump out for God that the Lord rewards and blesses immensely. It's interesting how in this Scripture, Simon Peter is the one to drag in the large net full of fish. I believe it's symbolic of the future ministry Peter would have.

One time I had a vision where I saw Jesus reach up in a tree and pick a fruit. He handed it to me and said, "Taste and see that I am good. It's yours to pick and choose to eat it. But eat it, and believe it. You are entering into a season now of walking in abundance and walking in ministry. I will flow with you as long as you move in faith."

My favorite saying from a dear evangelist friend of mine is, "Faith is spelled R-I-S-K."

Lord, let us be a people today who will risk everything for You. Let us jump out of our comfort zone.

Will you stretch your level of faith?

44

In Every Season, Trust

JUST AS THE EARTH ROTATES AND HAS DIFFERENT SEASONS, SO I HAVE learned that there are seasons in our spiritual lives with God. There are seasons when God calls us to battle. We rise up as His warrior Bride and wield our weapon of the Word and worship against the enemy's arrows and pray through our circumstances until the answer comes.

And then there are seasons to run. God opens doors like a flood gate that otherwise seemed closed. We run out in faith with Him into new territory and are challenged by His question, "Do you trust Me?" We are stretched beyond our limits and caused to grow new wings as we expand with Him. We set our focus and never veer off the course He has set for us. We give Him the glory no matter the pain, the sweat, and the tears that go into the process. Then we access the victorious side of the finish line, and think back, *Whoa, God, You really just did that; You really brought me to where You said I would be!*

And then there is a season to rest. We surrender beating our wings and learn to soar with Him.

One day I was outside with my daughter and I looked up and saw an eagle soaring through the air. Suddenly, the presence of the Lord came like a shifting wind. As I kept watching the eagle fly, I heard, "They gain power by soaring. It's a restful, peaceful, and powerful dance they do with Me."

"Be still, and know that I am God" (Ps. 46:10). Easier said than done, right? There are days when, as my circumstance doesn't shift, I can begin to wonder, *Where are You, God?* It's about being able to rest in the storm. To find the peaceful eyes of Christ and keep our focus on Him as we stand right in the middle of that tornado, and trust. Our love for Him is what grounds us, and His promises give us the faith needed to stay the course.

Nothing can hinder or hold back a fully surrendered person whose heart fully loves and trusts God, no matter the circumstance. We surrender our hearts, lean into Him, rest in our trust, and embrace the faith walk with Christ.

Be still. Be still and know that He is God. He's got you; you can trust Him. With an open heart, open your arms just as an eagle soars, and declare, "I surrender and I trust You."

> *Trust in the Lord with all your heart and do not lean on your own understanding. In all your ways acknowledge Him, and He will make your paths straight* (Proverbs 3:5-6).

45

Persevere

THERE IN FRONT OF ME WAS A DOORKNOB. THIS TIME IT LOOKED brassy, a little different from others I had seen. I could feel coolness on the other side of the door. I was entering a room in Heaven. I turned and looked at Jesus, waiting for His permission to enter. He smiled and nodded at me in approval.

Pushing the door open, I was instantly hit with a cool breeze. The air felt refreshing and new, like the fresh start of a day. Walking forward, I was outdoors with landscape as far as my eyes could see. I searched around, trying to capture everything I could see of the beautiful landscape in my memory. Trees of various sizes painted the horizon. Beautiful lush green grass squished between my toes. As soon as I saw the grass, I quickly kicked off my sandals to walk barefoot! Larger, more denser forest was up ahead off to my right. I curiously squinted hard, trying to see what might be inside that forest.

Jesus suddenly jogged up alongside me. "Come here. I want to show you something," He said. He ran up ahead and I quickly sprinted after Him. We ran ahead a few yards until I found myself near the entrance of the thick forest. Abruptly He stopped and stooped down to the ground. "Come look!" He excitedly called to me.

I bent down really low until finally I was lying on the ground, my face next to His looking. And then I saw it. In the dirt, a tiny spurt of green had pushed its way up through the dry, baked ground. It had persevered to live and gather sunshine.

"You see," Jesus said, as He pointed from the little seed sprout up to the giant pine trees that grew tall and seemed to dance in the sky up ahead, "small starts can produce great things. Those who take leaps must learn to soar. Keep your eyes on Me."

Let not the enemy take away your significance with God today. What you are doing *is* significant to Him, no matter how small it may feel or seem. From stopping to wipe the runny nose of a precious little one, to leading major corporation meetings, you are significant to Him. The start of a new dream can feel overwhelming and intimidating. You may have a net of encouragement, or maybe even no one at all to cheer you on, but persevere you must!

> *Do not despise these small beginnings, for the Lord rejoices to see the work begin...* (Zechariah 4:10 New Living Translation).

46

Keys of Worship

To my surprise, as I looked around the room that night, I saw actual musical notes falling from the sky. Worship was phenomenal that night at our church service. Both my husband and I felt like we stepped into a new level when one particular singer began to release a new song. The Spirit of the Lord was so present in that meeting.

When I opened my eyes during worship and glanced around the room, I was so surprised to see musical notes falling. The sound of Heaven was responding to our praise. Oh what it will be like to some-day to be right there with the angels and elders worshiping the King, *"Holy, holy, holy is the Lord God Almighty!"* (Rev. 4:8). Our worship unlocks the supernatural. Our offering, or worship to the Lord, is a key in shifting the atmosphere.

When I was in a hotel in Colorado, I was attacked by a spirit. I know to always pray over the hotel rooms I stay in, from anything evil that could have been left behind there. This spirit was there to harass me with fear. I declared Scripture and began to sing worship songs. As I released the sound of worship, that demon began to shrink and shrink, until it finally vanished. The presence of God then filled that room. When Light comes, darkness must flee.

This morning I was praying for a man over the phone who was from South Africa. As I was praying, the Lord gave me a picture of Joshua and his army marching around the walls of Jericho (Josh. 6). I could see them marching, blowing their trumpets like an alarm, and then the walls came shattering down with a loud, crashing sound. The sound was so loud that it actually startled me. I then heard the phrase, "Sound the alarm; release the offering of worship." So, I started singing in tongues over and over the South African man. As I sang, the healing presence of the Lord came over his back. His back became warm and he could feel the heat of the presence of the Lord on him. After a year of tortuous back pain and kidney problems, this morning he was released from pain and healed. *Praise God!*

We often can overlook the power of worship. As Jesus is facing temptation from the devil, He uses the Scripture, *"It is written, 'You shall worship the Lord your God and serve Him only'"* (Luke 4:8). Worship is our most powerful weapon. Our worship not only releases a sweet offering and fragrance to the King, but it causes the enemy to resist.

Will you worship Him today? Release the sound of your worship, and think of it as if blowing those trumpets that caused the walls of Jericho to come down. *He is worthy!*

47

Washing Basin

I FOUND MYSELF IN A ROOM IN HEAVEN THAT WAS DIFFERENT FROM previous ones I had visited. I saw a giant, porcelain bathtub in the center of the room. Although there were other items in the room, I could not take my eyes off that tub. For some reason, I just knew that the tub had something to do with why the Lord had brought me here. I could feel the presence of God radiating from it.

"Why am I here, Lord?" I asked out loud.

Jesus led me toward the washing basin. "Ana, do you trust Me?" He paused to give me time to search my soul.

"Do you REALLY trust Me?" He pressed the question again. "Really?" He paused. "Do you trust Me with the core of your being?"

I knew the answer to the question. Many things in my life I trusted to God, but there were a few areas I still held on to. A few matters of the heart that I reserved for myself. Issues floated to the surface that I was scared to trust God with. I realized that old wounds and the pain of disappointments had caused me to put up a guard with God. By holding them back for myself was my silly way of thinking that I would avoid disappointment again. Really though, I was holding myself back from all that He wanted for me. I wasn't allowing Him full access.

Then He looked me straight in the eyes, "Ana, rest from your distrust. Let Me wash you clean of it today. Allow Me to take residence in that area of old pain. Let's recognize what fear is there."

As I sat and pondered, Jesus sat patiently with me as I dug up the roots of my fears. Pulling up roots can sometimes be a long and painful process, but this time with Jesus was not like that.

He waited patiently as I self-examined what fear I was believing. He showed me how small, old wounds had created cracks in my foundation of faith. The enemy used those old cracks to sneak through and attack me, poking through the old wounds. I hadn't realized the cracks were so easily exposed.

I nodded to Jesus. I was ready now to shed the fears, like the scaly, old skin of a snake.

I stepped into the wash basin fully clothed, and Jesus came behind me with a giant cup in His hands. He poured a cup of oily substance over my head, and it ran down, soaking my hair, head, and all my clothes.

"Ana, you were allowing the enemy to imprison you to fear and bondage. Tonight I wash you by the power of My blood spilt for you, and command the fear to be rinsed off."

After allowing some time to pass by, He smiled and asked, "Will you trust Me, Ana?" His eyes looked me right in the face again. The invitation was serious.

"Yes, Lord, I trust You," I readily responded this time.

I pray that out of his glorious riches he may strengthen you with power through his Spirit in your inner being (Ephesians 3:16 NIV).

48

Stretched for God's Glory

When He had finished speaking, He said to Simon, "Put out into the deep water and let down your nets for a catch." Simon answered and said, "Master, we worked hard all night and caught nothing, but I will do as You say and let down the nets" (Luke 5:4-5).

GOD'S COMFORT LEVEL, AND OUR COMFORT LEVEL ARE TWO COM-pletely different things. I love this Scripture passage in Luke 5. Simon and the fishermen had been hard at work all night, trying to make a decent living. This wasn't just about catching fish because they were hungry; no, their income depended completely on their ability to fill their nets. After a frustrating night, they came up with empty nets. Then Jesus asks them to simply let down their nets again.

"Are you kidding me?! That's what we've been doing all night!" (I'm paraphrasing here, but you can almost hear Simon's frustration.)

But obediently they let down their nets again and caught the largest fish haul they had probably ever caught.

"I'm calling you up and in," I heard the voice of the Lord say to me once. The Lord showed me then in a vision a pair of wings. They were being stretch outward and then upward like putty in the hands of God. I watched, and as they were being stretched, they grew larger and stronger.

He was inviting me into intimacy, to be stretched for His own glory. I was facing an extremely "stretching season" of life. The thrills and trials of being a brand-new mom were leading me into a feeling of complete failure. Many late nights coupled with sleep deprivation brought lots of insecurities to the surface, and I was feeling pretty defeated. Ever feel like that?

No matter the circumstance you find yourself in today, look up toward Him. That season of life caused me to look up more to Him, and also press into Jesus with all of my being when I felt like I had nothing else to give. When I had no more strength, I found Him.

When Simon is stretched beyond his plans and beyond his own strength, He trusts in God and brings in the most fruit. His faith muscles were stretched.

Are your faith muscles being stretched today? "I'm calling you up and in," I hear the voice of the Father saying to you.

He gives strength to the weary and increases the power of the weak (Isaiah 40:29 NIV).

49

Tell It to Go!

HAVE YOU EVER ROLLED OUT OF BED IN THE MORNING AND THOUGHT, *Wow, the enemy really hates me.* It was one of those mornings. I had just returned home from teaching at a conference in Kansas City, Missouri, and the next morning I woke up to searing pain in my uterus. It literally felt like something was squeezing it tightly and twisting it—like wringing out a towel.

Moaning and throwing back the sheets, I mustered up the strength to make it into the shower. With the hot water pouring down my back, another searing pain shot through my uterus again.

"Why, God?" I asked in tears and agony in the shower. "Why am I hurting? What is this attack about?"

I heard no response. I prayed, but in all honesty, my prayers were more of a begging for God to take the pain away. All day I struggled to even move from the bed to eat. I ate mostly out of necessity, not out of want or desire. The mere taste of food made me nauseated as the pain was increasing and increasing.

The next day I decided to go see the doctor. After many tests and questions, the doctor came back with results, "Nothing. You have nothing wrong with you. Your tests came back showing that you actually are in perfect health."

Right then and there I heard the Lord's voice say, "I never told you this was something physical. You've always known this was a spiritual attack."

Later that night the pain and ache continued. As I laid down and could bear it no longer, I heard from Holy Spirit. "You don't have to be afraid of demonic attack. Don't give the enemy more power than he deserves. You can cast it out. Tell that pain to go."

Really, God? I thought. I had prayed all day, tried everything I knew to do, and yet the pain continued. But I hadn't yet simply told the pain to leave. So with the little faith I could muster up in that moment of pain, I laid my hand over my uterus and prayed, "Pain, go. I just command all the pain and attack that is over my body to stop now, in Jesus' name. I claim the blood of the Lamb."

Just like that, it left.

Now, if only it was that simple every time! There are days when I forget the power in my prayers. I forget the power and authority my God carries that lives inside me. Those days my circumstances beat me up, and I feel like the end of an old, used broom. But every now and then, I muster up the mustard-seed faith I need. That little ounce of faith that says I will prevail. Then I persevere and push through whatever circumstance—in faith I find His light and grab it.

I encourage you today, whatever your prayers are, He does hear them. You will prevail. Keep pushing and pressing into Him. Have faith! Have hope!

> *It is like a mustard seed, which, when sown upon the soil, though it is smaller than all the seeds that are upon the soil, yet when it is sown, it grows up and becomes larger than all the garden plants and forms large branches...* (Mark 4:31-32).

50

Into His Robes

He is clothed with a robe dipped in blood, and
His name is called The Word of God. And
on His robe and on His thigh He has a name
written, "KING OF KINGS, AND LORD
OF LORDS" (Revelation 19:13,16).

"Tuck me in, Lord," was my prayer that day. I was in a season of dryness; a season where it felt like the Lord was far away from me. I wondered many days during that season, *Where are You, Lord?*

Ever been there yourself? A season of dryness hits you, and you begin to wonder, God, are You close? Do You know what I'm going through here? Well, what do You have to say about it, Lord? Will You help? Do You really care? Are You really that big? Are You really that faithful? Will You come through for me TODAY, God?

I'm sure everyone has faced these questions with the Lord at some point in their lives, or maybe you are even posing these questions today before Him.

In that moment of desperation to hear from Him in my dry season, He spoke to me, "Come up here, beloved."

Instantly, I was taken into a vision. I saw Jesus seated on a large chair. He was beautiful. He was joyful, and love radiated through His eyes to me. His presence took my very breath away. I was seated on the ground, with my viewpoint looking up. I saw His sandals and His feet. I saw His flowing robes—white linen, covered with layers of purple and maroon cloths that were thick and soft. I couldn't take my eyes off those layers of robes for some reason. They flowed what seemed like forever, layer upon layer.

Then Jesus did something surprising. He beckoned me to climb up onto His lap and sit with Him. I climbed up onto Papa's lap, and He tucked me into the folds of His robes. I could feel the warmth of His chest as I leaned in. I felt peace come over me in that moment, and had total clarity of my thoughts. I gained perspective on the situation I was going through that day. I felt the Lord's presence and strength come over me in a renewed way as I was tucked in.

May you climb up into those loving arms of your Papa Daddy Jesus today. May you embrace His strength to face whatever mountain is before you. From grace to grace may you grow in the ways of His nature. May you lean into Him as your strength, love, and support.

51

Set the Beat

I was there in Heaven seeing before me a whole battlefield. I was marching. Why am I marching? I thought. There before me was a clash of power. I saw the enemy's workers sending out assaults against the King's soldiers. I saw the Lord's warrior angels fighting the demonic forces to protect the King's beloveds there.

As the battle thickened, my spiritual ears opened and I could hear the sound of battle: the clash of swords upon swords, shields smashing against armor, shrieks of pain as people's bodies were wounded by the enemy's arrows and claws, and also shrieks as the demons were stabbed and overcome by the King's army. Back and forth, back and forth the battle continued.

Then there was a loud alarm. The sound was disgusting! Surprisingly, I felt instantly nauseated when I heard it. It was unlike any earthly sound I have ever heard. Then, for a swift moment, I saw him. I saw the enemy seated on a nasty-looking beast, and then his image shifted away. He could move and change formation with ease. After that moment, I couldn't trace him with my eyes, but I could feel his presence still there leading his army. But he was hidden from my sight.

When that alarm sounded, I felt terror pulse through my body, so much that I couldn't move. The King's army scattered in disarray. As soldiers were separated from the group, I saw how they became more vulnerable to the enemy's attacks. Smaller demons rose up and could pick them off, one by one.

Then I heard the King's voice, "Time to release the drummers, Ana. Set the beat. Give the direction for My beloveds. We've gotten off course. Shift your focus. We are winning! Find the beat of My heart. Find the pulse of Holy Spirit and stay with it. Rise up. Grow louder in your declarations and prayers. Don't you know the power of prayer! As you step into the authority My Son has given to you, the sound of Heaven is released."

So then, there I was marching in the frontline of battle, carrying a drum. In the natural, I have no idea how to play the drums. I actually can't carry a rhythm! But here I found myself in Heaven, setting a beat. I was hearing the sound from the Father, and repeating it back on my little instrument. It was slow and steady at first, and then as the army of Christ joined with me, it grew LOUD and faster! Our sound broke louder than the clash of the enemy's assaults. And we grew strong! As I learned to tune my ears to listen more to the sound that the Father was making, than the battle that was happening before me, I could match His beat. We became victorious as we matched His sound.

Today, may you hear from God with clarity. May your spiritual ears be opened to catch what He's saying. May His voice become louder than any battle before you. And may you rise up to release the sound of Heaven!

...In the world you have tribulation, but take courage;
I have overcome the world (John 16:33).

52

His Eyes

Straightening up, Jesus said to her, "Woman, where are they? Did no one condemn you?" She said, "No one, Lord." And Jesus said, "I do not condemn you, either. Go. From now on sin no more" (John 8:10-11).

Wow. That moment. Can you stop and just imagine that moment when Jesus stood up after writing in the dirt, and looked at the adulterous woman, destined to be stoned and cast out. Then God intervenes. He looks at the woman caught in adultery. Their eyes meet. In that moment I wonder what she felt. Was she struck with fear thinking, What will He say? What's going to happen to me? Will He truly just let me go?

You can feel the tension that she must have felt. The overwhelming feeling of relief, as one by one each person dropped the stones and walked away. What was Jesus writing? We have to guess. And then her Savior stands up and looks at her. Their eyes meet, and in an instant, her understanding of love is magnified. She is free.

The eyes of Jesus. They stop me in my tracks every time. No matter what prayer I am bringing before the Lord, no matter the circumstance I am going through, those eyes—they demand everything to stop and adore.

I have had the privilege to look into the eyes of Jesus a few times in my life. Full of life, His eyes look more alive than anything else. Compassion and love radiate from them in such a way that seeing Him always melts me to tears. I am challenged to embrace the love of the Father; as I look into Jesus' eyes, I feel I am so undeserving of His love.

His eyes are an invitation. There is so much excitement in them. They always seem to say, "Will you come? Will you come be with Me? I want to show you something." There are healing waters, I have seen as I look into Jesus' eyes. Times when I have been under attack, I have seen Jesus in a vision; and as our eyes meet, as I stare into His eyes, sickness melts away.

Imagine a scale—on one side is deep friendship and on the other side powerful authority. This is what I've felt as I stared into His eyes. It's the perfect balance. My reaction is almost always the same, "Let me be slow to speak, Lord, and quick to love." And His response is always the same, "I love you. Oh how I love you."

53

My Room Prepared

THERE ARE MANY TIMES WHEN JESUS HAS TAKEN ME UP INTO HEAVEN and shown me different rooms. The encounter usually always begins the same, although how I am led there is different. I always find myself walking down a wonderful hallway in Heaven, with Jesus hand in hand. He leads me to a specific door and we either go together into the room, or sometimes I am asked to go alone. There I am blessed to encounter and see the wonders of Heaven. There is always a lesson for me to learn from the room He leads me to enter. The rooms always have a very specific purpose.

One day was a little different. I had been worshiping Jesus in my living room, when I suddenly felt the exciting presence of Holy Spirit in the room. I heard the Father whisper, "Come with Me," and suddenly I was led up into an encounter.

Hand in hand, Jesus and I walked down the long hallway. We passed some familiar doors, and others that were completely new to me. One door in the hallway caught my attention. It was a beautiful turquoise color mixed with tones of aqua and ocean blue. I loved that door! I was instantly drawn to it because it displayed all the colors I love. Even the pattern and design of the door's wood, I loved.

"Is this for me?" I asked Jesus.

"Yes. This is your door," He simply responded.

"My door?" Never had I experienced a door in Heaven that was specifically designed for me. My personal door—this was a new concept.

We entered through the door into a beautiful room. I laughed in joy as I noticed that filling the room were all the hobbies and things I enjoy. There were pictures of the ocean lining the walls. There was even a bag of beautifully colored yarns and knitting needles in one corner of the room.

I noticed a large easel set up in the center of the room with two paint brushes and two pallets with a variety of paint colors on them. Jesus and I started painting together.

I painted, but kept a watchful eye on Jesus to see what He was painting. *What will He make?* I kept thinking. *What is He trying to teach me through that picture?* I wondered.

Stopping and looking me in the eyes, Jesus put down His paint brush. "I'm bringing you into a season to create. It's not about the product here, but just be with Me. Together we will create. You are learning to co-labor with Me."

Then He moved toward me and touched my arm. Very seriously, He looked intently at me and said, "You've been working out of strife, even in your relationship with Me. You've lost your joy. That's not living in freedom. Let's do life together. Let's spend time together and just enjoy. That's real relationship."

I stepped into a new level with God. It wasn't about just knowing the authority and power of Him, but about knowing Him as my Friend. Too often it's easy to get lost in how to achieve deeper relationship with God out of a striving mentality. What do I need to do to go deeper? What do I need to do to gain more?

Jesus tells us, "Just be with Me. But really *be.*"

54

My Army Is
With You

*For He will give His angels charge concerning you,
to guard you in all your ways* (Psalm 91:11).

*Then Elisha prayed and said, "O Lord, I pray,
open his eyes that he may see." And the Lord
opened the servant's eyes and he saw; and behold,
the mountain was full of horses and chariots
of fire all around Elisha* (2 Kings 6:17).

THERE WE WERE, EYE TO EYE, KNEE TO KNEE. JESUS HAD BROUGHT me to a beautiful garden. In an instant, I found myself sitting and looking into the eyes of the King of kings, my Savior. Our knees touched, knee cap to knee cap.

"Hello, friend," He smiled and said to me. I was speechless.

He hugged me affectionately as I would a best friend. I was touched that He called me His friend. Being that close to Him felt so overwhelming. Zeal mixed with excitement, fear of the Lord mixed with awe and reverence, all seemed to leave me without words.

"I want to show you something," He said with a twinkle of passion beaming through His eyes.

We walked hand in hand to a large willow tree. As He pulled back the curtain of leaves, there behind the tree's umbrella were hundreds of angels waiting. Their brilliance and strength terrified me at first. Light illuminated and encompassed them brightly. I fell to the ground as I felt the power of God in this holy place. I saw the angels look toward Him, waiting for Jesus' instruction.

Jesus said to me, "These have been assigned to you. They will travel with you. They will defend you at times when the enemy tries to hit you with his arrows. Like a fortress, they will be. My army is with you."

He paused then continued.

"Don't forget this. There will be times when you will feel alone. You will wonder where I am. I pray that in that moment your eyes will be opened to see the army released to fight for you. Remember this."

You beloved, are not alone. He is for you, not against you. May you know Him as your Jehovah Nissi—your banner and protector, covering you on all sides.

55

Find Me in the Fire

FIRE CREEPS, DOESN'T IT? STARTING WITH JUST A SMALL FLICK, A small flame is ignited and then it grows and grows. There are seasons I have walked through that feel like the favor of the Lord is showering down on me. Life happens with ease and joy. Everything goes well and with purpose and I'm gaining momentum. And then there are other seasons when it feels like a huge fire is showering down on me unexpectedly. It catches me off guard and tries to swallow me and steal my faith.

One morning I woke up to a fire. The kids had become deeply ill while on our family vacation in another state—far from home and our family doctor. In the midst of scrambling to care for them, my husband became ill with the exact same sickness and was prisoned to his bed. Days of exhaustion with little to no sleep as the full-time nurse for the family left me in a desperate state with the Lord. "God, speak to me, please. HELP!"

I woke up that morning—day three of this rigorous battle—and felt the nudge of the Lord to go to the beach to rest. Let's be honest here. I'm not one to quit or back down when the enemy strikes! But I felt the nudge from God, "Get away with Me, just for a moment."

Laying down my battle plan for the day, I packed my backpack and headed out to see what God had for me.

As I walked on the beach, white sand squishing between my toes, the peaceful sound of the waves crashing to my left, I saw something in the distance that looked peculiar. There in the distance, someone had left a circle of drift wood standing straight up in the sand. *That looks weird, God,* I thought. Just a glance at it prompted me to wonder what weird ceremonies had perhaps occurred inside that circle.

"Enter in, Ana," I heard Him say. Reluctantly, I walked into the middle of the driftwood circle, feeling a little silly.

Suddenly, fire surrounded me on every side. I had walked into a ring of fire in the spirit. Everywhere I looked, surrounding me I saw the fiery, burning presence of the Lord. I took off my sandals quickly, following Moses' reaction when he stood on holy ground (Exod. 3:5).

Then suddenly, the Lion of Judah's face appeared through the flames. "I will protect you. Find Me in it all. Find Me, and hold on to your faith. A fixed focus will be your anchor. Find Me," He said. He brings me into right standing. In the firing, I can find peace and an unwavering worshipful heart.

That was a strong word I heard that day from the Father. He is our wall of protection through the moments of firing. But, there is a testing. Will you fix your eyes on Him through it? He is your Restorer and Strength-Giver, as long as you keep turning to Him through it all.

> *"For I," declares the Lord, "will be a wall of fire around her, and I will be the glory in her midst"* (Zechariah 2:5).

56

Not Just for Others

I was sitting at a healing conference one Saturday afternoon having a funny conversation with God. I had been sick with a stomach flu for the past few days, and just overall not feeling like my normal energetic self.

I was on the prayer ministry team for the conference. Funny, you might think, but there are many times when I have preached, ministered, and prayed for the sick and have seen God pour out His healing on others, while I am actually going through weakness. God uses the broken too, as long as we're willing.

As I was sitting there having a not-so-spiritual conversation with God about my feeling weak, I looked up and saw an angel on stage. The angel was riding a white horse and carrying a banner for healing. The banner didn't say the word "healing" on it, but it carried the anointing and fragrance of peace and healing that I have learned to recognize.

God's about to pour out, I thought to myself.

Then suddenly I was in a vision. I was sitting in Papa Jesus' lap. He looked at me and said, "Touch this," as He held out His palms and I saw the holes, which took me back a little at first.

"It's OK," He reassured me, "It won't hurt Me. You can touch them."

Reluctantly, I put my fingers in the holes. Immediately the power of God hit my body, and I felt His presence from head to toe renew me with energy and strength.

"Healing is for you, too. It's not just for others," He smiled and said.

> *But he was pierced for our transgressions, he was crushed for our iniquities; the punishment that brought us peace was on him, and by his wounds we are healed* (Isaiah 53:5 NIV).

Often the enemy hits us with discouragement. We see others get healed and we rejoice and celebrate with them, but we don't get our healing. It's almost as if we were passed over and another was chosen, or at least this is the lie that the enemy tries to strike at us with.

May the hope of Christ be your anchor today. May your thoughts be renewed and restored with the truth that "Healing is for you, too."

57

Starving for God

*And the temper came and said to Him, "If You are
the Son of God, command that these stones to become
bread." But He answered and said, "It is written, 'Man
shall not live on bread alone, but on every word that
proceeds out of the mouth of God"* (Matthew 4:3-4).

WHAT ARE YOU FILLING YOUR SOUL WITH TODAY?

A challenging question, I know. I was challenged by it too when
God asked me the question. I had been meditating on this portion
of Scripture in Matthew, and I heard God whisper and ask me this.

The question carries depth. It can't be overlooked or quickly
brushed away. It is a reality check for me even now, and hopefully for
you, too.

As I pondered the Lord's question, He approached me with another
thought-provoking statement and question: "Starvation can be in the
mind. Are you starving?" I heard Him ask.

Me, starving? I'm not physically starving right now, I thought
to myself. I knew, though, that He wasn't talking about physical

starvation in that moment. As I wrestled with this question, the revelation came. My soul was starving indeed.

What I normally knew to hold on to as an anchor for my soul—the Word of God—I had neglected to eat or ingest that week. Busyness and other agendas had filled my schedule, and it was leaking out onto everything around me. My mind was cluttered. My soul was starving for God.

It's interesting how the soul works. What we feed it produces an outcome, whether we realize it or not. For example, have you ever been around a stressed person or in a stressful environment and when you leave that environment, you feel more stressed than before?

If we have Jesus, we carry Light into dark places. But to be an atmospheric shifter and not shifted by the atmosphere itself, *we have to be grounded in His Word.*

So today, choose to feed your mind, soul, and spirit with the Word of God. Get still and get real with Him. Find Him in the clutter of life and let Him be your anchor.

58

Muzzle of Offense

WILD HORSES RAN PAST ME AT AN INCREDIBLE PACE. THEIR MAJESTIC strength was a little frightening at first. The enormity of the beasts running at a close distance, stopped me in my tracks. What was I to do? Do I run away or stand still so they don't hit me, was my predicament.

God, where have You taken me now? I thought, a little panic-stricken. This encounter with the Lord was unlike any others. God used animals to speak to me that day.

To my relief, the wild horses galloped by me, leaving me untouched. I stood mesmerized by their beauty. With each step, beams of sunlight danced across their powerful muscles. What struck me most was how truly free they were! They ran and galloped about, kicking up sand all around them. Some tossed back their heads and neighed in excitement. At times, some choose to be still and dip their heads down for a scrumptious sampling of the delicious grass beneath their feet. Others ran with a clear direction in mind, then suddenly shifted direction all together quickly.

Then I saw it. There was one horse I noticed off to the side of the herd struggling to run. He was isolated a bit. As soon as my eyes caught sight of this poor beast, he looked at me and walked sluggishly toward me. Unlike the others, this horse wore a black muzzle over his mouth and nose. As he approached me closer, I saw the word "OFFENSE" written across the muzzle.

I heard then the Lord's voice, "I have called the Body of Christ to know freedom. To love and receive love freely, and to run with Me. You're in it for the ride with Me. You can't have anything restraining you. Offense is a restraint to receive My glory. It will block the flow. Offense holds you back from all that I have for you."

That was the first time I had heard the phrase, "Offense blocks the flow," and it kept ringing through my head.

How about you today? Is there anyone in your life who has offended you recently? The enemy will do anything he can to try and block our connection with God. Let's do everything we can to remain full of love and without offense.

> *If I speak with the tongues of men and of angels, but do not have love, I have become a noisy gong or clanging cymbal. If I have the gift of prophecy, and know all mysteries and all knowledge; and if I have all faith, so as to remove mountains, but do not have love, I am nothing. And if I give all my possessions to feed the poor, and if I surrender my body to be burned, but do not have love, it profits me nothing. Love is patient, love is kind and is not jealous; love does not brag and is not arrogant, does not act unbecomingly; it does not seek its own, is not provoked, does not take into account a wrong suffered, does not rejoice in unrighteousness, but rejoices with the truth; bears all things, believes all things, hopes all things, endures all things. Love never fails* (1 Corinthians 13:1-8).

59

Finding His Wind

And He rode on a cherub and flew; and
He appeared on the wings of the wind
(2 Samuel 22:11; Psalm 18:10).

I FOUND MYSELF TUCKED AWAY IN THE CLEFT OF A ROCK. THE LORD had taken me up into an encounter with Him. The opening of the rock was narrow, but I could see out. As I peered out, I saw God's presence pass by quickly. Like a bright light with warmth beaming from it, so passed the presence of the King. I felt then a huge gush of wind that sent goose bumps rising up all over my body.

Then He spoke, "There is power in My fire, My light is My glory, and My wind is My peace. This is your season to know My peace!"

Later that day, as I was contemplating what Jesus meant by *"know My peace,"* I saw a small eagle physically land near my car. It was odd at this time of year to see this young bird. I watched it as it soared above my car for a while, before it landed. God showed me in that moment how eagles do not beat their wings, but rather find where the wind current is, and drift in it.

"OK, God. You've got my attention," I said out loud.

God wanted me to find peace and soar. Previously, when I had thought about the word "peace," in my mind I had referred to it as something to attain in a chaotic environment.

God was teaching me that finding His peace correlates with finding Holy Spirit's movement. It's funny, though, as I know Holy Spirit to be somewhat chaotic sometimes—like when Holy Spirit falls on a meeting and people burst out in abrupt laughter. Or the power of God falls in a meeting and people start falling down right and left under His glorious presence. Holy Spirit is like organized chaos, which is part of God's nature.

Peace is being OK with the flow of God, remaining flexible as He changes direction in our lives, or leads us down a different path from the one we started. Peace is about letting Him lead. His currents lead me, and I just hang on for the ride of my life.

Peace is about trusting His leadership—that His leadership is always good. Peace is about letting go of control and leaning into Him for understanding. Peace is about believing that He will hold you up, even when the ground feels like sinking sand in your life.

May He be your peace today. May you be comfortable in His directional flow.

60

Lay Them Down

CERAMIC POTS AND JARS LINED THE SHELVES OF THE ROOM. I FOUND myself that day walking into an old ceramic studio with Jesus. I could see the spinning wheel and a little stool pulled up beside it. A dirty apron was folded beside the stool.

I wonder what the Father is making?

Jesus led me to the shelves. One by one, I peeked to see which beautiful vessel He would pull from the shelf. He went to a shelf with older vessels sitting on it. I could see that these were not shining as radiantly as the others, as dust coated their once lustrous appearance.

Jesus went over and began to blow the dust off them. As He blew, I sensed that what He was doing was a prophetic symbol. Then He picked up one of the larger bowls. Dusting it off first, He then presented it to me. "Taste new fruit," He said with no further explanation.

Then I heard the Lord say, "Take off your sandals, this is Holy ground." So I removed my flip-flops, and I saw that I was now near an altar.

"You will bear much fruit in rest. Rest is a place of trust. Trust Me that I've got them. Lay them down. I'm dusting off your disappointment," I heard the voice of the Lord say.

I instantly knew that the Lord was talking about some people I had been praying for with great concern. Situations in their lives shared little to no hope in the natural.

Glancing at the altar, I knew why He brought me here. I knew what I had to do.

"I choose to give them to You, Lord. May You carry their burdens. I trust You Abba," I prayed as my tears dripped down the front of the altar.

Trust isn't an easy act. It's laying down your own will to control a situation. We do our part, and then it's up to God to do His. No matter the outcome, no matter the timing, we trust that He has a plan, and that His hand is directing the situation.

Sit for a moment and ask Holy Spirit to reveal right now if there is any bit of striving the Lord wants you to let go of today. Ask Him to show you if there is any burden He wants to carry for you today. Will you hand it back to Him, knowing that He is a good Father? Will you rest in trust?

> *Cast your burden upon the Lord and He will sustain you; He will never allow the righteous to be shaken* (Psalm 55:22).

61

Performance Spirit Broken

I HAD AN AGENDA FOR THAT DAY. FOR MANY YEARS, I HAVE BEEN searching for a special ring from the Lord. I believe that rings are important and symbolize covenants. So, I have been asking Jesus for a ring for a very long time, and I was on the hunt for it.

After much time wasted looking, I heard Jesus tell me to stop looking, and just head to a specific beach to hear from Him.

As I walked toward the beach, a specific tree caught my attention. It stuck out as unique and different from the others. Its bark was a brilliant red, and the red color seemed to run down it in stripes. I was staring at it when I heard the Lord speak profoundly, "My blood covers all and runs for you."

As I kept looking at the tree, I saw how the red coloring actually looked like blood trickling down the trunk.

Then God did something spectacular and unexpected. In an instant, He broke a performance spirit off me. I felt something that had rooted way down suddenly lift off me, and I knew in an instant what it was.

He brought me back to the freedom of the cross. He showed me how I had a real root and stronghold in my life in the form of a performance spirit. He showed me how many times I would carry myself throughout life, through trying to perform or gain acceptance, and how it even affected my relationship with Him. I had carried it into our relationship, trying to gain love, when I already had it to begin with.

Then He said, "You can't find your ring, because you did not understand its significance until now. This ring will be a covenant of freedom and love for you. It symbolizes that you are My daughter and are loved and accepted. It's a covenant of acceptance. Let My love fill you again. There's nothing you need to do to gain My acceptance; just be.

"I have crushed and broken that need to perform. I am calling you out to walk in love and wholeness. Your heart will expand greater for others now, because you love yourself. You will not set these past standards on others, needing to perform to receive love and grace. Grab onto *love*. Grab onto grace. Feel the wave of My presence now wash over you."

Just like that, a total wave of His glorious presence hit me. Warmth and tingling shot through my body, His glorious presence was over me.

Guess what? I then found my ring!

As you are reading this, you may be thinking, *OK, but what does this mean for me?* Stop and ponder for a second. Ask yourself, *Do I ever struggle with feeling the need to perform? Do I ever feel like I have to do something to get love? Do I have unrealistic standards that I set for myself? Do I ever struggle with criticizing others, or even criticizing myself? Am I hard on myself? Do I weigh too much of my self-value on other's opinions or acceptance? Do I feel like I have to have it all together, or else?*

If you find yourself answering yes to any of these questions, then perhaps you may be struggling today with an oppressive performance spirit.

May you believe in the power of the words *"It is finished"* (John 19:30). In Greek, this phrase Jesus said as He took His last breath is *tetelestai,* also written on business documents to show that a bill has been paid in full.

PAID IN FULL. His blood was enough. By the power of the blood of Jesus Christ, may you be set free of a performance spirit now. You are accepted.

62

In God We Trust

THE UNITED STATES OF AMERICA USED TO BE BASED ON THE PHRASE "In God we trust." It was the core of the country's founders. It's scary for me to wonder if one day this phrase will be eliminated from our currency.

I was walking to my car from the Bethel Church's house of prayer in Redding, California, when I noticed a shiny quarter glimmering on the ground, right next to the driver's side car door. Picking it up, as I love to find change, I noticed the phrase IN GOD WE TRUST on the quarter.

It seemed like God was trying to get my attention.

A huge transition was coming for my husband and I. We felt God directing us to leave everything we knew, leave everything we had established and that felt "normal," and move overseas to be missionaries.

I had just spent the past hour with the Lord, in a beautiful little prayer room, asking my questions about what the future would hold. "How will You provide for us, God? Will we have children overseas and build a family there? What would that even look like? Is it forever that You are asking us to move overseas? What will our future ministry look like, God, etc."

The questions rattled on and on, and to my disappointment, the Lord remained silent. And then leaving the prayer house, I found this quarter. Looking at that phrase now shimmering in my hand, I responded, "OK, God, I get it. I'm Yours."

Fear has many different faces. Fear of the unknown, can grip us in our seats. The possibility of being stretched beyond our limits and doing the incredible with our limitless God feels unreachable. But trusting Him opens a world possibilities—all within your reach.

Will you choose to be stretched today? Chose to trust Him. He's got you!

> *O Lord, You have searched me and known me. ...*
> *and in Your book were all written the days that were*
> *ordained for me, when as yet there was not one of them*
> (Psalm 139:1,16).

63

Dancing on His Feet

For an answer Jesus called over a child, whom he stood in the middle of the room, and said, "I'm telling you, once and for all, that unless you return to square one and start over like children, you're not even going to get a look at the kingdom, let alone get in. Whoever becomes simple and elemental again, like this child, will rank high in God's kingdom. What's more, when you receive the childlike on my account, it's the same as receiving me (Matthew 18:2-5 The Message).

I CLOSED MY EYES, AND THERE BEFORE ME I SAW IN A VISION JESUS' feet. Right there were my King's feet right in front of mine! I placed my bare feet on top of His warm feet. Then looking up, I saw His hands reaching down to grab mine. I was so much smaller than Him. Like a child, reaching up to grab onto her daddy, there I was. As I reached up, He took my hands in His hands and gripped them firmly.

"Let's dance, my beloved," I heard Him say. Together we danced in circles together, and as we danced I felt penetrating love warm my heart. We danced until we arrived before a set of large gates that were shut.

Smiling, He looked at me and pulled a set of golden keys out of His pocket. He found a key, that was a perfect fit, and turned it to unlock the giant gates that opened into Heaven.

Turning, He smiled and said to me, "The key is for you to keep your joy. My joy is your strength, so you must press into me right now. Let Me carry you, so that the enemy cannot steal your joy."

He then lifted me up onto His back—a piggy-back ride from the Father—what better way to play could there be!? He leaned back and I held on tightly, and then He spun quickly around. Like a child, I laughed with glee and He chuckled too. It felt so good to laugh with the King! It felt good to play as a child. It had been a long time since I had played.

God loves to have fun! Joy is part of His character, and it's so often overlooked as the powerful tool and weapon that it is.

Can you be childlike with Him today? Can you see yourself now, sitting on His lap, resting on Him like a child? Can you see yourself placing your feet on top of His feet today, letting Him lead you? Where will He take you? Somewhere glorious, I'm sure!

64

Access to the Throne Room

You know when you're reading through the Scriptures, and one particular verse seems to pop off the page at you? It grabs your attention and causes you to pause and chew it over. That's a "Holy Spirit moment"!

Reading through my Bible one day, I came across a passage in Zechariah that gripped me.

> Now Joshua was clothed with filthy garments and
> standing before the angel. He spoke and said to those
> who were standing before him, saying "Remove the
> filthy garments from him." Again he said to him, "See,
> I have taken your iniquity away from you and will
> clothe you with festal robes." Then I said, "Let them put
> a clean turban on his head." So they put a clean turban
> on his head and clothed him with garments, while the
> angel of the Lord was standing by (Zechariah 3:3-5).

And then following, I found myself right there in the throne room of the King. I saw the Father God seated on a mighty throne, at a distance. I could only catch a glance of Him, for the power and glory that was radiating from the chair was too strong. Fire and light mixed with warmth poured out from the altar. I fell on the floor in worship, as the power of God struck my body in immeasurable amounts.

I saw others seated next to Him, who I imagine to be the elders. They were regal. Small crowns adorned their heads, and their robes were of elegant colors. The presence of the Lord was all over them. They smiled at me, but said nothing.

Angels were all about the room, some right around the altar, others placed on guard. Multitudes of people were there as well, all worshiping the King.

I felt a little afraid. I had always dreamed of this moment. I asked the Lord many times to bring me here; but now that it was happening, I couldn't physically stand in the room. The amount of glory that poured out in that room was unlike anything I have ever experienced. All I could do was slightly lift my head to see the bottom of His robes that seemed to fill the entire room.

A loud voice boomed, and the King stood up. Addressing me, I looked up into His eyes as He spoke.

"Go back out and take off those garments. There are no beggars in Heaven. You are not a beggar! You are My heir. Go put on your royal robes and then you can come back."

Just like that, I was back sitting on my couch, my Bible still open on my lap, and I was covered in sweat.

I am His heir; I am His heir, I kept repeating to myself. A mindset was broken off me that day, and has forever changed the way I see myself and my relationship with the Father.

You and I do not have to beg God. He loves to bless His children. Often, as we don't receive the answers to our prayers in a timely fashion, we can almost get angry with God. We can catch ourselves wondering, *If I'm an heir truly, then where is my miracle? Where is the answer, God?*

Today, would you put on your royal garments?

It's a mind-set, not just a physical act of wearing royal clothes. It's stepping into knowing who you are to Him, knowing the power and authority you carry because you have the living Christ inside you. It's knowing that regality carries responsibility, and knowing that He hears you and values you—whether or not you feel it in the moment.

We cannot base our grasp of His love upon the moment. Rather, let it bear witness to our souls today, that *we are not beggars.*

You, beloved, are His heir!

65

Pressed

RECENTLY, I WENT THROUGH A ROUGH SEASON. I FELT LIKE I WAS being pressed on every side. Have you ever been through a season like that? I think we can agree that when we're in those seasons, we can't wait for the ending to be near. We look forward to the finish of the hardship. In my weakness, I met with God tonight to discuss my current situation. That's what I thought the agenda was for the night; God had other plans, though.

I prayed, "God, what are You doing right now?" And, He answered.

I suddenly saw that I was before a large circular press. As I drew near it, I could see it was in fact an olive press. Olives were inside the large stone contraption, and I watched as they were being squished, oil being separated from the rest of their contents. I kept watching the large stone pressing and squishing those olives over and over. I didn't like that stone! The process seemed quite barbaric to me.

Then as I stared at the olives being squeezed, I heard His voice, "I'm pressing you right now. I'm turning up the heat. What will be extracted out of you during this season? What will be the sound you release? Will you still exhibit my joy, love, peace, patience, kindness, gentleness, and self-control? Will you still trust Me, and say that I am good? I love you, and I am here, but you must know it even when you can't feel Me. I am not distant. I will take care of you, but you must do your part. Praise me. Press through the pain and worship and watch what I'll do through this. I am for you, not against you. The pressing is a refinement of your character. You will see what's in your heart during this season, and you will see how much you truly need Me. Come, let's do this together."

All too often, when I'm facing something hard in life, I just think about getting through it. It's about the product, right, not the process? Wrong. "Process" is a word a lot of us don't like, the same with "refinement." God loves me just as I am in my broken state, but He sees the potential. The process doesn't scare Him, otherwise He would have turned away long ago from humankind.

You may be being pressed right now. If so, out of this refinement season, will rise the sweetest perfume and fragrance in your life. You will grow beyond what you thought you could, but you will be stretched.

So will you choose to worship, worship, and then worship again today? I am convinced that sacrificial worship releases the sweetest aroma to the King. He's right there beside you in the pressing seasons, and He's proud of you.

> *But about midnight Paul and Silas were praying and singing hymns of praise to God, and the prisoners were listening to them; and suddenly there came a great earthquake, so that the foundations of the prison house were shaken; and immediately all the doors were opened and everyone's chains were unfastened* (Acts 16:25-26).

66

Emotions Anchored

I SAW A BOAT CAUGHT IN THE MIDDLE OF A HORRIBLE STORM. THE little boat looked as though it would capsize and be taken down under. Wave after wave crashed and beat up against its sides. As the waves beat down, a cracking sound of the structure of the boat being broken apart echoed across the storm.

That's how I was feeling right then too, and perhaps you're in the same place. God took me up in a vision this day to encourage me, but as I heard that sound, I felt all the more discouraged in that moment!

"Why are you showing me this God? You know that's how I feel right now. I am like that boat! I don't know how much more I can take right now."

Just then I saw the Father's hand drop down and lower a giant anchor. The anchor crashed and plummeted through the intensity of the waves. The waves rose up and resisted it. I could see the battle going on between the storm and the anchor, but the anchor cut through it all. It was dropped through the waves, and immediately the boat shot upright and leveled out. Then a supernatural peace came over that little boat. The storm continued, it didn't cease, but that little boat stayed grounded.

"I am internally grounding you," I heard the Lord say. "I will be your peace in the storm, your comfort, and your anchor. I am holding you firmly grounded in Me, even in the midst of the storm. Let not the enemy steal your peace. My hand is upon you."

Just then I felt His peace. It's not like my situation changed instantly, but my outlook on it did. All the emotional storm I felt in relation to my circumstance ceased, and I felt peace. Peace in the storm.

I think about the story of Jesus asleep in the middle of the storm.

Jesus Himself was in the stern, asleep on the cushion; and they woke Him and said to Him, "Teacher, do You not care that we are perishing?" (Mark 4:38)

If you're like me, you might wonder, *How in the world did Jesus sleep in the middle of that storm. It's not as though He was unaware of the storm going on!* As the disciples moved quickly to fear and panic as they thought their lives would be over soon, Jesus slept. His emotions were unmoved by the storm. He was grounded in peace and trust in the Father.

So today, would you be challenged to anchor your emotions with the peace of the Father and trust in Him in every circumstance? Declare today, "You are my anchor, God, and I choose *peace.*"

67

Bring Them Here

I FOUND MYSELF BEFORE A LARGE WASHING POOL. IT LOOKED UNLIKE a modern-day pool, more like a giant bird bath. An intricate design of seraphim bordered the pool and twinkled with a slight touch of gold.

"Where I am, Lord? What are You showing me now? I wondered.

The pool looked inviting, so I decided to jump in fully clothed. Immediately the water felt warm to the touch and full of His presence. Hearing a sound, I was distracted from my current fun of splashing in the Father's presence.

I looked up to see angels walking toward me, leading others toward the pool. I smiled at the others coming to the pool, but when they came near, they stopped, like they didn't know what to do once they got there.

"Come in," I called out to them.

Still they stood by the edge waiting for something to happen.

I looked at an angel, as he smiled back encouraging me. So I jumped out of the pool and grabbed the first man by the hand. I led him to edge and showed him how to get in and then splash around and enjoy the presence of the King. And then I went and grabbed the next person and helped that person into the pool.

Then suddenly I was sitting on my couch in my living room, journal still open in my lap. What an interesting encounter with the Lord that was.

Out of that encounter came the following prayer, and I dare you to pray the same prayer boldly today.

"Lord, would You make me a person who helps others find Your presence. I don't want to ever get comfortable and selfish in Your presence and keep it all for myself. I want to bring others in. I want to help others find You and find freedom. Would You let me assist people in getting washed clean from whatever might be holding them back from getting in touch with You. Lord, let my own home be a place where Your ever-flowing presence would dwell. Let my home be a place of refreshment and encounter for all who visit. I don't just want to sit by the side of the pool waiting to perhaps get a little sprinkle of Your presence splash up on me. I'm all in, God. Let me swim and encounter Your presence today. But let me bring others here too, Lord. I want to show others who You are and how much You love. For Your glory. Amen."

68

Last-Minute Healings

RECENTLY, A DEAR FRIEND OF MINE BECAME EXTREMELY ILL. THE disease that was wreaking havoc upon her body came with ferocity and moved quickly. It was quite shocking. I was asked to come pray for her.

As I laid my hands on her that day and began to pray for her healing, the Lord opened my spiritual eyes and showed me an incredible vision that proved to be quite prophetic for her.

I saw my friend clinging onto the edge of a mountain ledge and climbing upward. She ran out of options of places to put her feet and push off. There was nowhere else she could reach with her feet to climb anymore. She was stuck. As she tried to reach out with her foot and find a place to grab onto, she fell off the ledge. As she fell, I heard her cry, "Abba!" and an eagle came right then, flew right beneath her, and caught her. She safely clung to the eagle's neck and flew away. The mountain she had been climbing burst with purple volcanic ash that filled the sky. Purple represented authority and being cleansed in the blood. I saw my friend dressed differently as she flew away. She was wearing priestly garments.

As I shared the vision I had seen with my friend, I told her, "God's gonna heal you, but it may feel like it is last-minute. You will gain a new measure of faith and authority that you will walk in. Your healing is coming, my friend!"

I wonder, is that you today? The Lord reminded me of that vision I had for my friend, and told me that it's not just for her, but that there are many others. You may need a sudden burst of encouragement, that refreshment of faith knowing that *He is coming, and He is healing you!*

Or perhaps healing is not what you need. You find yourself relating to being on a ledge climbing, but unable to find a strong place to step up. You find yourself wondering, *Where are my options, God? What else do You have for me? There has to be more than this?*

You will know this word is for you, because as you are reading it now, the Holy Spirit will start to stir within you. He is coming! He is the God of surprising suddenlies. Trust in Him. May you receive healing now, if you need it, to every cell of your body. May you receive hope and a new outlook on life. May He make your path clear and direct in every way, and show you the next step He has for you. Although He may not show you all the steps in between the greater picture, just trust Him for the next step, and then the next, and then the next. Let faith arise. He is coming!

> *Yet those who wait for the Lord will gain new strength;*
> *they will mount up with wings like eagles, they will run*
> *and not get tired, they will walk and not become weary*
> (Isaiah 40:31).

69

Invest in People

GARDENING IS PERHAPS MY MOTHER'S FAVORITE THING TO DO IN THE whole world. I always tell her, "Mom, someday in Heaven you're going to be attending the Father's roses!" While I still see the labor of gardening and not the joy in it, she always assures me how refreshing it can be. I have no green thumb or huge desire to test out my gardening skills, but one day the Lord took me into a garden in Heaven.

I was taken up in a vision where I saw a path amid a garden. Both sides of the path were lined with rose bushes. Other flowers and plants were there too, all of various colors and sizes. There was a joyful buzz in the atmosphere in The Garden. I kept walking the path until I heard humming and recognized the voice. Turning a bend in the path, I came upon Jesus joyfully watering His plants, watering can in hand. Did you know Jesus is happy? He is so full of joy.

He looked at me and smiled. "Come help Me garden, Ana," Even if He wasn't all-knowing, although He is, the look I gave Him in response could have said it all.

Um...but I kill plants, Lord, was the thought I responded with apprehensively.

He laughed in response to my thought. "Come here, I want to show you something," He said joyfully.

As I approached Jesus closer, I could see that He was actually watering the ground now. Looking down curiously to see what kinds of flowers He was so interested in, I gasped as I saw an open window. There I saw us above the earth below, and Jesus was watering down on the earth. I could see specific people's faces and the Lord was watering them. I could see the people drinking in His presence in absolute refreshment. I watched as Jesus joyfully watered the people below, and then continued to water the rest of His Garden.

Then just like that, He was gone. I was still there looking about His Garden when I heard His voice. "Will you water My Garden? This is your season of pouring into people's lives. You may not see the growth right away, but let not that discourage you. You are ministering to My heart by investing in people. You see, you're matching the heart of the Father. Invest in people, Ana, not for them, but for Me. People are always worth the investment. Love them, show them My love. I will always replenish what you pour out. But do pour out."

> *And He said to them, "Come away by yourselves to a secluded place and rest a while."* (For there were many people coming and going, and they did not even have time to eat.) *They went away in the boat to a secluded place by themselves. The people saw them going, and many recognized them and ran there together on foot from all the cities, and got there ahead of them. When Jesus went ashore, He saw a large crowd, and He felt compassion for them because they were like sheep without a shepherd; and He began to teach them many things* (Mark 6:31-34).

70

Untangling Destiny

For the vision is yet for the appointed time; it
hastens toward the goal and it will not fail.
Though it tarries, wait for it; for it will certainly
come, it will not delay (Habakkuk 2:3).

THERE I SAW THAT ALL TOO FAMILIAR CORD BEING UNTANGLED again. The cord was like a strong rope with many strands running through it. Knots aligned the cord, breaking up the smooth uniformity of the braids. I saw the Father's hands come down, and start unraveling it again. He was weaving a new design. There was a strategic plan and purpose with every move He made, and I just sat back and watched in wonder. *What would He throw my way this time? Where was He taking me now?*

It's not all the time, but every so often the Lord will take me into an already-experienced vision again. I revisit it, and the Lord gives me deeper revelation each time. This was one of those visions. At strategic times in my life, the Lord has shown me this cord, and His unraveling and reworking it. I will be in my prayer time with Jesus, and then suddenly I will see that cord and His hands

153

grasped around it. It's always a great reminder to me that the Lord is behind everything.

As I watched and wondered what the strategic realignment of those strands could mean this time, I heard the Father's voice, "I am realigning things in your life, like this cord. Everything that has been preparing you is like a stage that has been planned for this moment. I am about to untangle some of the knots and give purpose and direction to you. You will have clarity and understanding."

There are things I have walked through in life that, looking back on it, I can now understand how God had a plan all along, even when I didn't understand it at the time. Like when I was in college and I felt a passion and pulling from the Lord to study and become a sexual assault crisis counselor. Now at the time, I had no idea why or where God would use that. I studied hard, worked for a rape crisis center, and gained a lot of skill, experience, and understanding. Then later God said, "Go to Brazil as a missionary." There I ended up working with former street girls, who, the majority of them, had gone through abuse in the past and were still walking through their healing. God had a plan all along. At the time though, I couldn't see it.

God has a plan for you. A friend of mine says, "If you have a pulse, God has a purpose for you," and I believe that phrase is true. No matter where you find yourself today, God has a plan and purpose for your life. Although you might not understand why you are going through what you are, or where God's purpose is in what you are currently doing, let me reassure you, His hands are always guiding and leading. He is behind you and beside you and knows your future.

71

No More!

I FOUND MYSELF PRAYING THAT MORNING FROM A PLACE OF FEELING defeated. Ever been there? Life hits you, and you feel like, "I don't know how much more I can take here, Lord!" As I was complaining...err...praying I meant, I saw a vision suddenly of Jesus leaning back in a chair.

So, I decided to do the same, and I physically leaned back and looked up. Instantly, I found myself seated at the Father's table in Heaven. There was Jesus looking back at me; His eyes filled with tears of compassion.

He said to me, "I'm so sorry you are going through this. This is a real assault on your family. You are about to turn a corner with this, but come and eat. Get refreshed."

There before me, I saw the most interesting foods. All kinds of fruits, breads, and foods I have never seen before on earth. After I finished eating, the Lord handed me a goblet of something that tasted like sweet, creamy milk. As I refreshed myself and drank from it, the Lord suddenly turned into the Lion of Judah. He approached me and got right up close to my face. I almost choked in that moment, startled.

He roared, "NO MORE!" right in my face. The power of the Lord hit me, and I felt the battle of the enemy was silenced and cut off in that moment.

I declare right now for you reader, that Jesus paid the full price on the cross for you and your family. You are covered in the blood of the Lamb. So enemy, you need to back off in Jesus' mighty name. The reader and I may feel broken right now, but *greater is He who is in us, than he who is in the world* (see 1 John 4:4). The enemy cannot break us down and cannot steal our faith and joy. I declare that you, oh reader, are stronger than you think. Not by your own power, but by His within you. You are not defeated! You are victorious! The Lord is calling you up to a new position of authority. He is giving you the strength now to stand as He did for me that day!

72

Friend to Friend, Heart to Heart

OUT OF COMPLETE FRUSTRATION AND FEELING DEFEATED, ONE OF MY greatest Heaven encounters with the Lord came one day. Whatever place you find yourself in today, I hope this encourages you and speaks to your soul. May you find intimacy with King Jesus today.

An angel came right up to my face. He came so close, that it took me by surprise and fear. He was a warrior angel, carrying armor ready for battle. The glory of the Lord that was in my face pouring off the angel, was so strong. Before I even had time to react, the angel blew a trumpet in my face and I instantly saw the Lion of Judah. He roared right in my face, and the power of it seemed to vibrate down to my soul.

He said, "No more. Anxiety and defeat be broken off of her." In that moment, I could see a literal spirit of anxiety being lifted off that had attached itself to me. I saw that the spirit carried a long cord, and as I wondered about that, the Lord said, "A generational lineage of anxiety and fear is being broken off of you right now."

Instantly, I felt my peace and joy restored. Fear had completely been lifted off of me. I then found myself in a room in Heaven where

Jesus and the angels were. I saw armor and mantles lining both sides of the room. The room seemed to go on forever. Jesus took me, hand in hand, and showed me my mantle again. I was taken aback by its beauty, almost as if it was the first time I was seeing it. A beautiful light-weight dress, lined with pearls, but tougher than steel, hung for me to see.

"Remember these pearls represent the times when out of conflict or storm you sought joy and praise. Joy is your weaponry, and you've forgotten!" He said.

Next, I found myself in a beautiful meadow. Holy Spirit was there in the form of a woman this time. "Come with Me," she said. "I want to show you something."

I found myself back in Heaven. I was in a room where Jesus was. His body was crushed, bruised, and almost unrecognizable from the brutality of the cross. It was horrible! I knew that somehow if I ever was allowed to see Him like that again (as I had seen Him once before like this), that this time I would reach out and grab hold of His wounds. I knew that I had permission this time. So with much courage mixed with fear, I went forward and reached out and touched the fleshy wounds on His back.

Instantly, I found myself taken into another vision where I was walking through curtain layers. I was being led by something, but I wasn't sure just what. As I pulled back layer upon layer, finally I peered through the last layer to find King Jesus. There He was in His glorified state, body completely healed. The magnificence that radiated from His very eyes, made me buckle at the knees and hit the floor.

He came to me as a deep friend then. He met me on the floor, grasped my hands and said, "Oh there you are. I've missed you. Here we will begin to meet, friend to friend, heart to heart."

73

Not a Worker

I WAS WATCHING CAROL ARNOTT MINISTERING AT BETHEL CHURCH via web stream one night. At the end of ministry time, she laid hands on a woman, kissed her forehead, and said, "Rest." As I watched her do this, the same phrase echoed deeply in my spirit and instantly the power of God fell on me in my living room. I found myself shaking under the power of God from head to toe.

Then I saw an angel standing before me. He was very tall, standing floor to ceiling. Fire came off his body, so much that I couldn't look directly at Him. A voice that seemed to come from behind the angel asked me, "What do you want?"

Shaking, I said, "Intimacy with You. To know You deeper. I wanna go deeper."

Then the response came, and may you take this today and receive any impartation that is on it as well: "Let the fear of the Lord be your strength. Come back to the place where you lay your head on my chest. Forget about producing for you are above that. You are not a worker but My love."

Then the angel was gone; just as sudden as when He arrived, He left.

I found myself repenting forever trying to strive or prove myself in my relationship with others, in relationship in my marriage, in relationship with my kids, and in relationship with God. I repented for getting so busy that I had forgotten to just be with Him.

Then I began worshiping and praising Him. As I sang, and I'm not the best singer, I felt the presence of the Lord fill our living room. I opened my eyes and saw the Lion of Judah right beside me. This time I wasn't afraid. He felt like a warm, inviting friend. I nestled into His hair and the Lion caressed me. I felt the warmth of His mane and I melted into tears in the presence of the Lord. God was teaching me about a season of rest and leaning on His chest.

> *John leaned back onto Jesus' chest. "There was reclining on Jesus' bosom one of His disciples, whom Jesus loved"* (John 13:23). *Mary got it too! "but only one thing is necessary, for Mary has chosen the good part, which shall not be taken away from her"* (Luke 10:42).

I don't know if you're like me, but sometimes I have found that even in my walk with Jesus, I can get to a place of striving to grow deeper with Him. I have to check my motives daily. Why do I want more of Him? Really. *Why?* If the answer to that question is not to be more intimate with Jesus and because I love Him, then I know I'm in a wrong place. I need to get back to the simplicity of the Gospel, and lean on His chest in adoration.

74

Swim into the Unknown

THERE I WAS STANDING BEFORE THE SEASHORE WITH ABBA. THIS time God came to me as the Father. Together we stood at the shoreline watching the waves crash one after the next. No words passed between us. This moment was sacred. I didn't want to say anything, but just be with my Father. We stayed there watching those waves for a long time, until the sun began to set.

Finally, He turned to me and spoke, "The time will be soon. It's coming. Hold your faith, that it is truly coming. It will be here sooner than you think."

He took a long pause, and I could feel the tension that was there. I knew in my spirit that something wasn't right. I heard the words He said, but couldn't feel peace about it. It's as though my faith just wasn't there yet to believe that the promise I had been praying for such a long time would be fulfilled.

Turning back to address me again, He looked lovingly in my face. "There is something you have to shed here today," He said, and then He was gone.

I faced the waves alone. As I stared in wonder and was asking Holy Spirit to show me what it was Abba was referring to, I saw that over my shoulders hung a cloak. It had the word "Fear" written all over it.

Just then Holy Spirit replayed to me an incident that had happened in my life. In it, I was allowed to see myself. I watched as I placed the cloak of fear over my own shoulders and used it as a comfort. It felt safe. Fear had become a nice shield to hide behind. What shocked me most as I watched this replay, was that it wasn't the enemy standing behind me placing that cloak over my shoulders, but in actuality it was me. I placed it there. I chose fear.

Ever been there?

I desired that promise of God for my life, but somehow it had become easier to just contend for it than actually BELIEVE it would come to be and declare it from a place of peaceful trust. Promises of God require action, don't they! We step into our promise, and it requires a change. Somehow fear had become more comfortable to me, to hide under this cloak than step into the promise. A fear of the unknown was pushed up into my face. *If that promise does come, then what, God? How will that change my life, because it will require a change.*

As I threw that cloak of fear off me into the ocean waves, I heard His voice. A joyful voice boomed, "Swim into the unknown! Let joy and trust be what you wear!"

> But Moses said to God, "Who am I, that I should go to Pharaoh, and that I should bring the sons of Israel out of Egypt?" And He said, "Certainly I will be with you" (Exodus 3:11-12).

75

Three Challenges

IN THE MIDDLE OF A WORSHIP SERVICE AT CHURCH ONE DAY, WITH my eyes completely closed, I heard the footsteps of the Father approaching.

Can you hear them? Stop a moment, close your eyes, and see if you can hear His footsteps approaching you. Maybe you don't hear them, but maybe you can see them coming closer. Take this opportunity to stop and wait on Him.

"Come with Me, Ana," I heard Him say.

I was then walking in a dry desert with the Lord. The heat was unbearable. As we walked farther and farther, I found myself gasping for air. The second a drop of my sweat fell from my body, it quickly evaporated. I felt like I was suffocating from the amount of heat steaming off the land.

As we walked, the Lord turned toward me, "Are you thirsty?"

"Yes Lord," I replied, and then He was gone.

I trudged up a hill of sand alone, wishing He would come back. Realizing how desperately I wanted Him there with me, I had new revelation of the Scripture that mentions being thirsty. No longer did I think about being thirsty as just being hungry for Him, but now I thought of it as wanting and needing to be close to Him. I longed for Him to be there with me, and I actually missed Him. Thirst in a dry, hot desert brings on desperation. In the same sense, I found myself desperate to be near Him.

Are you thirsty?

As I kept trudging along, suddenly I the environment completely changed before my eyes. Where the ground had once been dry, grass rose up, and the environment resembled a lush valley. A river ran through it, and trees lined the river, their branches full of leaves.

I quickly walked toward the water, ready to quench my thirst.

"Will you remember to give Me the praise in the lushness as well?" I heard Him ask me.

The question challenged me. Often I find I have it backward— praise God when life seems dry, but when life is flowing well, I forget to turn around and praise Him for it. In every season, praise the King.

As I made my way to the river's edge, the scene changed before me again. I saw a land full of old bones. Heaps of bones piled up all around me. Disgusted, I thought, *Lord, why have You taken me here?* Then Jesus appeared to me and asked, "Do you believe I have the power and authority to make this a land of the living?"

Quickly responding to His question, "Yes, Lord," I spurted out.

He paused then asked, "But do you believe that in My name, you can do the same?"

My faith was instantly put to the challenge.

> *These three challenges have stuck with me and continue to work on my character. Am I truly thirsty for Him, not just for the power, signs, and wonders of God* (although wonderful), *but desperate to be near Him; desperate to be close? "My soul thirsts for You, my flesh yearns for You"* (Psalm 63:1).

164

Will I continue to give God praise not just when things are tough, but when blessings flow? Will I turn around and praise the One whose hand is behind the nozzle? Will I give Him *all* the glory?

> *"Were there not ten cleansed? But the nine—where are they? Was no one found who returned to give glory to God..."* (Luke 17:17-18).

> *Will I believe truly that the Christ I carry inside of me is bigger than any mountain? "...he who believes in Me, the works that I do, he will do also; and greater works than these he will do..."* (John 14:12).

76

Jesus as a Comforter

ALTHOUGH GOD IS ALWAYS REFERRED TO AS A FATHER, ONCE JESUS came to me as a mother figure, and comforted me. The following is the encounter I experienced.

There I saw Him. Abba was sitting, rocking in a chair in a warm living room. A fireplace crackled in the distance, keeping the two of us toasty. The room was thick with the Lord's presence. I could sense Holy Spirit bustling about the room, although I couldn't see Him.

"Come sit, Ana," Abba beckoned me to sit on His lap.

As I sat down on His lap, He reached his arms around me and pulled me into His chest real close. The hug was unlike anything I had ever experienced with God before. The hug felt nurturing, similar to a mother comforting her child who is in pain. He held me for a while and rocked and rocked. There was nowhere else I ever wanted to be, just there in those arms in that moment. He was healing me, just by holding me like a nurturing mother.

After some time had passed, He spoke words that unlocked my repressed tears, "You matter to Me! I see you. It's OK in this moment to just feel. Allow yourself to be held right now. I love you just the same when your emotions are negative, too. It's OK now. You can let it out. You are safe. You don't have to hold your breath anymore. You can just be. I love you."

Like a broken dam, the tears started crashing down my face. He was healing me.

Today I pray for you, reader, as you come across these words on the page, that they would minister to your soul at whatever place you are in your walk of life. May you find God as a Comforter and Nurturer. You can just be. He loves you just the same.

> *There is no fear in love; but perfect love casts out fear...*
> (1 John 4:18).

77

Map Room
in Heaven

I will instruct you and teach you in the
way you should go; I will counsel you with
My eye upon you (Psalm 32:8).

WOULD YOU BELIEVE THAT THERE IS A ROOM IN HEAVEN FILLED with maps of your life? Once God took me to the map room in an encounter, and since then I have been back several times.

I was reading through the Scriptures one day, when I had an open vision. I was suddenly soaring through Heaven, seeing red and purple glory clouds. I reached out and grabbed them in my curiosity. As I kept soaring, suddenly I saw a door before me. There was Jesus waiting at the door. Together we walked through the door and entered into a large room.

I saw there angels bustling about the room, carrying large, rolled up papers that looked like scrolls. They were carefully searching the shelves, that lined the room on each side, for specific scrolls, then gathering them up and placing on the large wooden tables that were all around the room. Papers upon papers were on the tabletops.

I watched as Jesus would take a scroll, unroll it, and then read the papers one by one. The angels stood by His side waiting for instruction. Looking at one with interest, He spent a little more time examining it. He then turned to a specific angel and motioned for him to come over and view the paper with Him. Jesus waved His hands about and gave Him instruction, and I just stood back and observed it all.

After the instructions had been given, turning to me He said with a smile, "Do you want to see yours?"

"YES, LORD!" I quickly shouted, and was led by an angel to one of the tables.

An angel handed Jesus a scroll. He carefully unrolled it and placed in on top of other papers.

I looked down and watched. I saw a map with many different countries highlighted with warm gold dust. It was blurry though, and hard to see where exactly I was to go with my husband. Trying to make sense of it all, an angel stopped me abruptly. The angel picked up the map and blew the sediments of the gold onto my heart.

I heard the Lord's voice, "Don't worry. The destiny is written on your heart. I will show you when the timing is right."

Know, beloved reader, that God has a plan and purpose for your life. He has carefully scrutinized over the map of your life and is leading you—whether or not you can feel Him in this moment. He is behind it all.

78

Restored Heart Value

TODAY, DO YOU KNOW HOW MUCH YOUR KING JESUS VALUES YOUR heart? This core understanding can completely transform your entire outlook on life and your purpose. I know it did for me!

Once I was led up to Heaven and allowed to see my own heart. There I found myself, walking into a room with Jesus. I saw a giant altar up front with bowls on each side of it. I looked at this altar with admiration, as I knew my own prayers along with others had filled those bowls as a sweet offering unto the Lord.

Out of the corner of my eye, I saw a small pedestal in the corner of the room. It was beautifully grafted, outlined in gold. Its design was truly marvelous. I could see something was sitting on the very top of it. Seeing my interest, Jesus nodded and encouraged me to come with Him to see what was there.

As we approached, I gasped in shock. It was a heart, a real human heart! *What's going on here, Lord?* I asked in my thoughts.

"It's yours, and it's beautiful," Jesus answered my question out loud.

I still didn't understand why He was showing me this. *But why is it there, on that beautiful pedestal?*

"I want to show you something more," Jesus said.

He motioned me to sit down with Him on some chairs beside Him, that I hadn't even realized were in the room until this point.

Just then, like a motion picture flashing before our eyes. I saw on the wall of the room, a story. It was part of my own story. I watched a scene unfold before me of something extremely difficult I had walked through in the past. Tears streamed down my cheeks as I watched it.

"Now, watch this," Jesus grabbed my attention.

Then I saw it. In the movie of my life, I saw myself, after that difficult event, walking into the altar room carrying my own heart. Instead of placing it on the special pedestal set apart for it by God, I laid it on the floor and walked away.

I was shocked. I never realized this is what my response had been, but it all made sense now. In that moment, I had devalued my very own heart. The Lord then went, picked my heart up, and set it on that special pedestal.

Did you know God places high value on our hearts? He sent His Son to die and go through the horrific reality of the cross, just because He values us that much. But do you? Do you value your own self? We are all in a process of working on our character daily with the help of Christ, but do you value the creation God made in you? Your heart is absolutely precious to the Lord. How do you care for something that matters to you? With care. How can you care for your heart today?

> *Are not five sparrows sold for two cents? Yet not one of them is forgotten before God. Indeed, the very hairs of your head are all numbered. Do not fear; you are more valuable than many sparrows* (Luke 12:6-7).

79

Everlasting Love

THERE IS A ROOM IN HEAVEN WHERE THE EVERLASTING LOVE OF THE Lord flows without ceasing.

I was in a dry season in my walk with the Lord. *Where are You, God?* was a common question of mine. Then God showed up. He took me into a vision. I suddenly found myself in a room that had what looked like water dripping from it.

As my eyes adjusted to take in everything I was seeing, I noticed something unusual about the flow of the water. The water defied gravity, and was literally climbing *up* the walls, then dripping from the ceiling and covering the floor. The texture of the water was more like honey. It was sticky and dripped in globs down all around me.

I saw a sink in the middle of the room and water was running out of the faucet. Being taught rightly by my parents to never waste water, I trudged through the water on the floor to get to the sink and turn off the faucet. The sink was full and overflowing. As I tried to turn off the flow of the water, I quickly realized that I couldn't. It was cemented open.

As I kept trying to turn it off, I heard the voice of the Lord, "You can't turn that off. This is My liquid love, and My love will never turn off."

As soon as I realized that this room was literally flooded with the love of God, I quickly ceased my task and dropped down to swim in the water. I wanted to experience as much of that love as I could.

Then I heard, "Don't forget this room. From here, you minister!"

Today, I pray that you will experience a new measure of the love of the Lord. May His presence come and penetrate you even now. Dare to swim deeper in His love today. We can always go a little deeper. Nothing you do will ever shut it off. It is everlasting.

> *Again he measured a thousand; and it was a river that I could not ford, for the water had risen, enough water to swim in, a river that could not be forded* (Ezekiel 47:5).

Living Out of an Orphan Spirit

And the Holy Spirit descended upon Him
in bodily form like a dove, and a voice came
out of heaven, "You are My beloved Son, in
You I am well-pleased" (Luke 3:22).

HOW MANY BELIEVERS WOULD LOVE TO HEAR GOD SAY HE IS WELL-pleased with us every day! Just as Jesus' ministry is about to take off, the Father first reaffirms Him in His love and how proud He is of His Son. How amazing is that!

One day I was in my prayer time with the Lord, and I heard Holy Spirit whisper, "I want to show you something."

Next I saw in a vision, a small child. Her eyes were full of fear and anxiety. I watched as she looked to and fro franticly from side to side looking for love. She was scared that love would be quickly taken away from her. Her body carried the posture of wanting to be closed off from the world as she folded her arms tightly, guarding her heart. The little girl was defensively protecting herself from anyone around her, as though she wore a sign, "Do not get close." Despite the Father standing right behind her, she felt alone, unlovable, and scared. The wounds she carried were completely visible, but she was trying to cover them.

Just then I heard the Father say, "This is an orphan spirit, and this is what most of the churches are operating out of today."

Isaiah 61:1 says, "...He has sent me to bind up the brokenhearted, to proclaim liberty to captives and freedom to prisoners."

While reading this and any of the picture that I saw and described resonates with you, know that the Lord truly wants you to be set free of an orphan spirit today. If you: feel jealous, struggle with insecurity, feel like you have to work for love or have a hard time receiving love, put unnecessary pressure on yourself, or live out of fear of what others might think, know that you might be operating out of an orphan spirit.

> I pray for you right now that an orphan spirit would be broken off of you and your generational lineage, in Jesus' name. I declare that you are not an orphan but rather you are "rooted and grounded in the love of Christ." That you may come to "know the love of Christ which surpasses knowledge, that you may be filled up to all the fullness of God" (Ephesians 3:17,19).

81

Promises Restored

...but the righteous will live by his
faith (Habakkuk 2:4).

...even God, who gives life to the dead and calls
into being that which does not exist. In hope
against hope he believed... (Romans 4:17-18).

"...Not by might nor by power, but by My
Spirit," says the Lord of hosts. "What are you,
O great mountain? Before Zerubbabel you will
become a plain..." (Zechariah 4:6-7).

THESE SCRIPTURES HAVE BEEN LIFELINES TO ME WHEN FACED WITH great discouragement or when my faith is shaken. I love where it says, *"In hope against hope he believed."* It encourages me that I'm not alone in having moments of lost hope or faith.

Sometimes life hits us, and the enemy tries everything in his power to shake our faith. Faith and trust are two of the most powerful weapons the Lord has given us. Whatever mountain might be standing in front of you now—maybe the mountain is unbelief that the promise will come to fruition—in faith you can declare that the mountain must bow down. Mustard-seed faith.

One day, I was faced with my own unbelief. My marriage is a very unique story. Ten years before I met him, the Lord showed me who my husband was to be. For ten years, I interceded for him, and had to stand on the promise of God. I had never met him, had no idea how I would meet him, and was not even pursuing finding him. I just prayed. Ten years rolled by, and I still prayed, but didn't have much faith left that I would ever find him.

Then one night, Holy Spirit woke me up with His gentle whisper, "Mustard-seed faith. Where is your faith, Ana? Do you still believe? He's coming." I was shocked. By now I prayed, but they were weak prayers lacking much faith for my husband.

Then the Lord showed me a vision. I saw the Lord walking around a beautiful land. This land, the Lord had previously showed me, represented my promised land from Him. So I saw Jesus walking around the land, restoring all the nooks and cracks that had been dried up. He placed His hands over the dried up, cracked dirt, and I watched as He breathed life into it, and the crack filled up and grass started growing there. He turned to me, with a smile on His face, and said,

"I am restoring your faith. Dare to believe again. I am healing years of the enemy's assaults over your promise."

Three months later, I met my husband in person. We both knew from that first meeting that we were each other's spouse.

I pray faith right now to be imparted to you. I pray for your faith to be restored today, that His promises are yes and indeed. If you have heard a word from the Lord, let nothing sway your faith in it. I pray the assaults of the enemy over your promise to cease now, in Jesus' name. Let faith arise!

82

Knee to Knee,
Eye to Eye

Come to Me, all who are weary and heavy-laden,
and I will give you rest. Take My yoke upon you and
learn from Me, for I am gentle and humble in heart,
and you will find rest for your souls. For My yoke is
easy and My burden is light (Matthew 11:28-30).

THERE I SAW HIM. THERE WAS MY KING JESUS, SITTING IN THE GARden waiting for me. He motioned for me to come sit down and join Him. So I sat before Him, knee to knee, eye to eye. For months we have met like this and have heart-to-heart conversations.

Today, I came with a question. Many things laid heavy on my heart that evening: I received an email from a lady who was sick with cancer and asking for prayer; I had been hit by slander all over the media; my husband and I were working through some marriage stuff; I had a conference coming up for which I needed to prepare; the laundry was piling up; my son was teething and therefore our whole family was not sleeping. The list went on and on. My heart was "heavy-laden."

And when Jesus beckoned me, I ran to meet Him. Knee to knee, eye to eye we met. Looking into those eyes, I instantly started crying. "How did You do it, Jesus?" I wept. "How did You balance it all? How did You keep Your joy and Your strength when You had the pressure of the world on You?"

After some time passed, I looked up into His eyes and was surprised, for His eyes looked at me tear-filled, too. "Lean into Me, Ana. This world will strip you. But you must lean in. Not by your strength, but by Mine. Look at me." He paused. "No really look at me!" He persisted.

I looked into His face and He said, "Keep your focus. Worship and lean in."

Just like that, I was back in my living room with my Bible still open. Those words and that encounter have sustained me more times than I can even count. When life gets tough and I feel completely beat down, I do those three simple things and am sustained, strengthened, and find supernatural joy beyond my circumstance.

- Lean into Him today. He will renew you.
- Keep your eyes focused on Him, not your circumstance.
- And praise Him in the storm, even when you don't feel it. Praise brings breakthrough!

83

Mixing Spices

THERE I SAW HIM BEHIND A GIANT MIXING BOWL. *IS JESUS BAKING?* I thought to myself in wonder.

It was a Friday afternoon, kids were napping, and I had a moment to put up my feet. As I opened my Bible for my daily read, my eyes latched onto this Scripture:

> *For the body is not one member, but many. If the foot says, "Because I am not a hand, I am not a part of the body," it is not for this reason any the less a part of the body. And if the ear says, "Because I am not an eye, I am not a part of the body," it is not for this reason any the less a part of the body. If the whole body were an eye, where would the hearing be? If the whole were hearing, where would the sense of smell be? But now God has placed the members, each one of them, in the body, just as He desired. If they were all one member, where would the body be?* (1 Corinthians 12:14-19)

Then He took me into an encounter. I saw Jesus standing at a counter mixing something in a bowl. Never before had I seen Jesus in a kitchen. He smiled at me and laughed at my curious look.

"What are You mixing?" I asked.

"Come see," He replied.

Approaching Him, I could smell what He was mixing before I saw what was in the bowl. Spices were being mixed together and turned over and over with His spoon. As Jesus rotated the spoon in the bowl, new fragrances were being released. The fragrances were amazing! Orange mixed with frankincense, rose mixed with an earthy smell, cloves, peppermint, and many more aromas that I cannot even describe were being released. I breathed them all in, as each odor was released at the turn of His spoon.

"I am mixing the spices and releasing a new fragrance over the earth. Each person has a part, their portion to bring to the mix. The new fragrance of Christ is being released."

And just like that, I was back on my couch, Bible still open on my lap.

Some think of "New Fragrance" as God releasing a new Bride, which is an exciting word for the upcoming generation. Yes, we want new and fresh fire and revival to spread across the nations! That doesn't mean, though that the older generations are discredited in this new fragrance being released. It's a beautiful mixture, you see. Every person has their part to play in this beautiful walk and love story with the King.

Whatever gift you carry is valuable to the King, even if you feel it is small or different from others. Be encouraged today, that what you carry personally, the mixture of giftings you have, the Body of Christ needs. Do something with what you've been given!

84

Carpet Time

ONE DAY THE LORD WHISKED ME RIGHT UP INTO HEAVEN. I WASN'T asking for it that day, it just happened. You gotta love the suddenlies of God! I was listening to worship music, headphones on, and then suddenly, bam! Just like that, I was walking with Jesus up in Heaven.

He smiled excitedly at me, and said, "I want to show you something!"

We then walked through a series of doors. The encounters I experienced in those rooms were amazing and far too difficult to explain.

There is one room, though, I feel I am to share. First, I heard the phrase, "Proverbs 8:21," which I looked up later.

Next, I was led through what looked like a courtroom. Jesus led me to the left, and there I saw a beautiful, exquisite carpet. I personally am not a huge fan of carpet, but this carpet was breathtaking. The colors were so radiant, it seemed to move. Hues of burgundy, purple, and gold swirled throughout every fiber.

I knew in that moment that it was a royal carpet. I was almost afraid to even touch it, based on how exquisite and expensive it looked.

Jesus smiled at me. And I thought, *Why are You showing me this gorgeous carpet, God? What's the meaning behind this?*

"I brought you here today to show you this. This is for carpet time," He said and then paused. "All the royal priests and generals have spent countless hours here! This carpet is for encounters."

So immediately I stretched out on the carpet. The presence of the Father fell all over me. It felt like I had sunk under water and was on the bottom looking up. That's how heavy the presence was all over me.

I heard His voice, "Stay close to Me, Ana. Invest time with Me. Be still and seek," and again He said, "Be still and seek. Fruit comes from adoration."

Then suddenly, worship bubbled out of me and I found myself singing, "In the stillness, in the stillness I know that You are near."

Later I went and looked up the Scripture I had been given at the beginning of the vision:

> I love those who love me, and those who diligently seek me will find me. Riches and honor are with me, enduring wealth and righteousness. My fruit is better than gold, even pure gold, and my yield better than choicest silver. I walk in the way of righteousness, in the midst of the paths of justice, to endow those who love me with wealth, that I may fill their treasuries (Proverbs 8:17-21).

Don't get lost in discouragement today, if reading this you are thinking, *But I've never seen a royal carpet like that.*

"Carpet time" is a great metaphor for us and reminder to seek Him and spend time with Him. It's not enough to just seek Him for the glory encounters, but to maintain glory and then impart it to others, we have to stay intimate with the One from whom the glory comes. It's out of our heart's desperate cry for more intimacy with Him that He meets our hunger with mountain-top experiences like Moses had (Exod. 34). Through intimacy, we then get to store up Heaven's treasures.

85

Not a Workhorse

"Workhorse." When I heard the word from Holy Spirit, it stopped me in my tracks.

"Look it up. Look up an image of a workhorse," Holy Spirit gently nudged me.

So, I headed to the library to check out an encyclopedia…just kidding! I did what most people do this age, I whipped out my computer and searched the Internet for an image of a workhorse. I saw a horse trudging along, plowing a field with heavy equipment attached to its back and with blinders on each side of its head so vision was blocked to only look forward. Seeing that image caused me to melt in a pool of tears. That was exactly how I felt!

The season of life I am walking in now is very full. With two little ones at home, a family to care for, a full-time ministry that keeps me traveling and preaching, often away from home, and a book to finish writing, I can often feel the heavy pressure on my shoulders to "just plow."

Ever feel that way?

Jesus took me on a journey that evening that was pretty impactful. I started thinking back to when life was easier. Was it when I just had one child? Was it when my family consisted of two—just my husband and me? Was it when I was single? Was it when I was overseas in missions? Was it when I was back in college, just studying?

I quickly came to realize that each season provided me the opportunity to complain and wish I was in a different place. I would plow through it, hoping that one day it would get better. It's not wrong, of course, to hope for a better future. But truth be told, what is your heart's attitude about where you are now? Can you have joy despite the season?

As I was reflecting on this, I heard Holy Spirit whisper, "You have felt defeated. Give those areas to me." Instantly, I thought of five main areas in my life that I kept working toward improving, yet always feeling defeated in each.

As I laid them down at my Savior's feet, I prayed a simple but empowering prayer, "Lord, I choose to lean into You with these areas that feel like trials somedays. I need Your strength. I am weak and that's OK, because You aren't! I choose to live life to the fullest, enjoy life, work hard, but not let it define me. I choose to love well, myself included. I will work hard, but not just plow through life and miss the joy of it."

I can do all things through Him who strengthens me (Philippians 4:13).

86

Free Indeed

Suddenly I found myself before the tomb of Christ. I had been worshiping the Lord with my headphones on, and just like that, He took me into a vision.

It was different from how I had always imagined it. For some silly reason, I had always imagined the outside of the tomb to be a lush garden scene, but instead I found myself walking in the dusty dirt toward an entrance to a tomb, a cave. The presence of God was strong there, so I quickly tossed off my shoes.

There He met me, outside the tomb. It was Jesus. He was radiating light and smiling from ear to ear. He was so joyous that laughter just bubbled out of me at seeing Him. I ran to Him and threw my arms around His neck, and He hugged me back.

After a while, I asked Him, "Should we go in the tomb?"

"No Ana. You don't need to. I am here, outside the tomb."

He paused, then continued, "I want you to hear and understand. Some are still living like they are in the tomb looking out. For them, the stone hasn't been rolled back, like I couldn't defeat satan. But I am here, outside. I am victorious—so are you. I want you to live like you're living from the victorious side of the cross. Believe and declare My words today, *'Nishlam.* It is finished.' Let's brush defeat off you today."

With that, Jesus gently touched my back between my shoulders, and I felt something lift off of me. Lightness, hope, and joy filled my spirit again. Where I had been feeling defeated that day, was now no more.

So if you are feeling defeated about something you're going through today, know this—He is not in the tomb anymore. Jesus resurrected. And as an heir of Christ, you can claim the victory of the cross.

Declare with me now:

- I am not defeated; I am an overcomer.
- I am victorious through Him.
- I am not a victim to the enemy's assaults against me, or my family, for I am covered in the blood of the Lamb.

87

Meeting My Son in Heaven

IT WAS ONE OF THE MOST SHOCKING EXPERIENCES I HAVE EVER GONE through. Just like that, after finding out I was pregnant with my first-born, only a few weeks after moving back to the States from overseas, I lost him.

Miscarriage is a horrible experience that many women (myself included) have gone through. Grief hits in a shocking way, as sudden loss fills your soul. Losing a baby leaves you with a sense of empti-ness, like something is missing. My world slowed down. Everyone around us seemed like they were moving in fast motion, while my husband and I experienced life in that season through a blur—a true symptom of grief.

God gave me the most healing and precious gift one day; I met my son in Heaven. I heard the Father's voice say gently, "I have something for you, My love," and suddenly I found myself in an encounter.

There I was walking on a beautiful path, lined with flowers on each side. The atmosphere was so peaceful and calm. A young boy suddenly came out of nowhere and took me by surprise. This boy seemed to be about the age of five (which I will never understand), and he looked just like me. He had my beautiful green eyes, sandy colored hair, and also my excited energy. I saw my exact smile radiated back at me through his face. He was my son, and I was shocked!

"Mom!" He called out to me, then came running and leapt up into my arms.

I cried in absolute joy at meeting him. "You're so beautiful, so handsome," I sobbed over him. I held him for what felt like forever, running my hands through his hair.

Finally, he said, "Do you wanna meet my friends?"

"Sure! Of course I do!"

Together we skipped hand in hand down the path. He took me to a specific room in Heaven where there were lots of angels. "These are my friends," my son smiled and pointed to a specific group of angels. "They look out for me." As he said this, an angel winked and smiled at me.

"See mom," my son said excitedly, "I like to play with angels too!" We both laughed at that together.

Next, he took me to a room filled with lots of children. All the kids were tuning their instruments, getting ready to play. Angels were there working with each section of the orchestra, helping the children. Adults were helping the band, also. My son smiled at me and ran off to join the orchestra.

"He's musical!" I said out loud with joy.

I dare to share this very personal story because I know there are many who have gone through the loss of a child. Or perhaps you have just lost someone who was very dear and close to your heart.

Seeing the joy that my son has in Heaven, and how happy he truly is there, brought so much comfort to my heart. It lifted the heaviness of grief I was experiencing. He's happy. He's truly in complete peace, protection, joy unmeasurable, and he is with *God!*

May your own heart be comforted today.

88

No Matter the Season, Hold On

THE LION OF JUDAH WALKED RIGHT UP TO ME. "JUMP ON," HE INDI-
cated. So without hesitation, I jumped onto the back of the Lion. I
grabbed onto His mane as He ran very fast. As a first-time rider on
the back of the Lion of Judah, He didn't give me a beginner's ease-in.
Together we soared over great plains, down valleys, and up mountains
until finally we came to the top of a precipice, overlooking the great
landscape below. Wind brushed hard against my face, and I struggled
to catch my breath after the great journey we had just experienced.

The Lion paused, sat down, and looked at me straight in the eyes.
The great fear of the Lord came over me in that moment. I knew
whatever He was about to say would leave a thumbprint on my life,
and I sat in the uncomfortable stillness, waiting.

After a long pause, He said, "You must learn to ride without reins!
Trust My ways, no matter the season. Grip onto me and never let go.
There are times coming when you will have to have a firm grip on
your position with Me. Do you trust Me, no matter what and no mat-
ter the cost? I climb every mountain, and I can strip them all down.
Have faith."

That conversation, is one that has stuck with me for a very long time. It's one that God has reminded me of many times.

Holy Spirit cannot and will not be restrained. This word God spoke to me about "without reins," doesn't have to do with not having restraint, respect, honor, accountability, etc. That all has its place in the church and is biblical.

"Without reins" has to do with His nature. God is the God of surprises. Can you stop and take a moment to imagine what Moses must have thought in the moment when God parted the Red Sea? An entire body of water was divided before the eyes of Moses and the Israelites.

> Then Moses stretched out his hand over the sea; and the Lord swept the sea back by a strong east wing all night and turned the sea into dry land so the waters were divided (Exodus 14:21).

I think my response would have been something silly like, "WOW, GOD! You just did that!"

Every time I think I know God, He surprises me and challenges my faith, and does something amazing. It's like He says, "Watch what else I can do!"

Riding without reins requires a deep trust of Abba, your Papa. No matter the season, no matter the circumstance, He's got you. There have been different seasons in my life when God has taken me into a similar encounter as riding the back of the Lion of Judah. Sometimes it's fast and exhilarating—a season where God opens doors, asking me to leap forward into the unknown without restraint and without looking back, fully trusting. Other times, I am just leaning on His mane, learning to rest and valuing the pursuit of deep, quiet intimacy and restoration with Him.

No matter the season, *hold on!* It's the best ride of your life, living fully surrendered.

89

Joy Unmeasurable

*Sing for joy and be glad, O daughter of Zion;
for behold I am coming and I will dwell in your
midst," declares the Lord* (Zechariah 2:10).

...in [My] presence is fullness of joy... (Psalm 16:11).

JOY IS VERY OFTEN OVERLOOKED IN THE CHURCH. BE HONEST. WHEN you go to a swirling Holy Spirit-filled service and people are drunk with the Holy Spirit, laughing on the floor, what's your reaction? *Is this really You, God?* Admittedly, I confess I was one of those skeptics.

Then I got filled with joy—*real joy,* truly from the throne room of God, and my life was changed.

It was a rough season my husband and I were going through in our marriage. We were in Mozambique, Africa, as missionaries. Missions has an interesting way of bringing out the best of a person—and also the fleshly worst. The daily challenges stretch you in ways you never even imagined being stretched!

I'll never forget it. We were invited to a special marriage-celebration-prophetic service; and in all honesty (I truly do love my husband dearly), in that moment I didn't even want to go with him. We had the opportunity to experience something amazing for our marriage, but as warfare often comes before breakthrough, that morning we were at odds with each other.

So there I was in our little living quarters before the event, complaining to the Lord. "I don't want to go to this prophetic thing, God. I don't even want to be there. I'm hurt."

Just like that, a twelve-foot angel showed up, and stood over me. Its presence knocked me flat on my back, landing me on the bed. It carried a large trumpet in one hand. Looking at me, it smiled, blew that trumpet right in my face, and declared, "The joy of the Lord is your strength!"

I felt that trumpet blast throughout my body when the sound was released over me. Guess what happened? I was so full of the joy of the Lord that my husband had to help me walk to the flatbed (our mode of transportation, similar to a large truck but not as luxurious!) that would take us to the event. As I literally rolled into the truck laughing, I layed down and touched the feet of my friends—other married couples going to the event—and the joy of the Lord splashed onto them. When we reached our destination, all of us tumbled out of the vehicle so full of the joy of the Lord—and so in love with our spouses.

Ever since that encounter with the angel, I have learned so much about the powerful weapon of joy! Times when I have seen the enemy come and try to bring division, discouragement, oppression, set people off course, depression, sickness, and offense, the enemy's weapons are defueled by the power of *joy!*

Hebrews 12:2 says *"for the **joy** set before Him endured the cross."* Take a moment and think on that Scripture. Joy helped Jesus endure the cross. Joy is one of the most powerful weapons He gives us!

So, how is your joy today?

Pray with me: "Holy Spirit, I ask You to come now and fill me up with joy. Head to toe, I pray for Your joy to come wash over me. I pray for my mind to be cleared of the day's trials, my body to be open and receptive to Your touch. Come, Holy Spirit. Bring new perspective through the lens of joy. Amen."

90

Promotion Through Service

HER FACE CARRIED PAIN. JUST LOOKING AT HER, I COULD TELL HER body was in torment. My husband and I were overseas at the time, in Nepal doing missions work with Iris ministries, and we were visiting one of the known-poor neighborhoods to pray for the sick that day. Poverty, injustice, and defeat united this little cardboard-box-and-tarp community of people.

Our translator motioned us to follow him into one of the tarp huts to minister. There we met her. Honestly, I can't remember her name, but her face I will never forget. Wincing in pain, she pointed to her stomach. Just like that, she lifted up her shirt and showed us her oozing stomach wound.

My honest first thought, *Oh no! I don't do oozing wounds, God.* (I know, not the most compassionate response in that moment.)

OK, God. What should I pray?

"Just hug My daughter. Hug her, like you are hugging Me," He said.

So, I did. I took the small Nepali woman in my arms and hugged her. She held on to me for what seemed like forever, but in reality was probably only three minutes. Holy Spirit told me to hold on as long as she wanted, which with a total stranger could have been awkward. I held on long and hard until she finally pulled away. With the most gorgeous big smile spread across her face, she looked at me; and in that instant, I saw Jesus staring back at me. It only lasted a second, but it was beautiful.

The King showed up in a complete stranger to me that day. Then pointing down to her stomach, she lifted up her shirt and revealed her completely healed wound to my husband and me. The Lord totally healed her that day through a simple hug.

Later that night, as I sat processing that healing testimony with the Lord, I had an encounter. I suddenly was in the Father's living room. A warm fire glowed. I was sweeping His floor, joyfully cleaning. As I looked down at the handle of the broom that was in my hand, I saw the word "Promotion." Then I heard His voice. "Spiritual promotion comes out of compassion and service. The fragrance of sacrificial love."

> *Heal the sick, raise the dead, cleanse the lepers, cast out demons. Freely you received, freely give* (Matthew 10:8).

> *Then He poured water into the basin, and began to wash the disciples' feet and to wipe them with the towel with which He was girded* (John 13:5).

91

He Never Said It Would Be Easy

HAVE YOU EVER HAD A PROMISE FROM GOD FOR YOUR LIFE, BUT FELT like every time you tried to walk in the direction of that promised land, you faced some sort of attack?

I found myself walking in a season of declaring my promise from God, but feeling quite lonely in it. The Lord asked me to author a book about the seer anointing, but the timing was most peculiar. I was fully pregnant, and yet God said, "Ana, now is the season to write."

I would sit before my computer, and almost every time I would go to write, I felt a block. I couldn't write, I couldn't hear God, and I was distracted in my thoughts.

So, I started increasing my prayers about writing this book. Literally, every time I would spend a morning prayer time pressing in for revelation for this book, declaring all the breakthrough and healing people would receive from reading my book, dedicating the book to the Lord, etc., then I faced spiritual warfare.

Sneakily, the enemy would hit me in different ways, so that often I didn't even recognize it was him. Fear spoken over me by people I knew, confusion in friendships and relationships, marital tensions, even fear of being left behind from ministry—you name it, the enemy would try and hit me with it all. The enemy used any tool he could to take my focus off of what God asked me to do, and also steal my confidence that writing is truly what the Lord asked of me. It never failed. Every time I wanted to write or intercede for my book, he would strike.

At a meeting I was attending one day, a prophet called me out in front of a large crowd, asking me to stand up. He said, "You have an assignment of the Lord on your life right now to write. Your book will set people free and also unlock the supernatural for people in new ways. You have to recognize the enemy is trying to set you off course. He's stealing your focus, and making you feel less than others who launch ahead in their ministries right now. But *this is your assignment from the Lord in this season!* You hear Him correctly! Recognize that the enemy wants nothing more than to stop that assignment, because it will bring people freedom and into the light of the Lord."

Labor pains bring out the strength in all women that we never realized we had. Right before the baby's grand appearance, the feeling of giving up tries to swallow us. Destiny is the same!

So maybe today you are feeling some push back from the enemy. I want to encourage you that perhaps you are very close to an incredible breakthrough. Those promises of God could be just right around the next corner. Push through it. Rebuke the enemy and stand on the promises of God you have over your life. If you don't have a promise yet, I encourage you to dream with God. Ask Him what He is calling you to do with your life, and wait for confirmation to roll in.

He never said it would be easy, but God promises to always be with you and carry you through.

> *What joy for those who can live in your house, always singing your praises. What joy for those whose strength*

comes from the Lord, who have set their minds on a pilgrimage to Jerusalem. When they walk through the Valley of Weeping, it will become a place of refreshing springs. The autumn rains will clothe it with blessings. They will continue to grow stronger, and each of them will appear before God in Jerusalem (Psalm 84:4-7 New Living Translation).

They wind through lonesome valleys, come upon brooks, discover cool springs and pools brimming with rain! God-traveled, these roads curve up the mountain, and at the last turn—Zion! God in full view! (Psalm 84:6-7 The Message)

92

Complain Not, Just Worship

*It is not what enters into the mouth that defiles
the man, but what proceeds out of the mouth,
this defiles the man* (Matthew 15:11).

*Open for me the gates where the righteous enter, and
I will go in and thank the Lord. These gates lead to
the presence of the Lord, and the godly enter there*
(Psalm 118:19-20 New Living Translation).

THESE TWO SCRIPTURE PASSAGES SPEAK MEASURES FOR THEMSELVES.
The Lord calls us to be very careful about what we speak out of our
mouths. One day in a vision, the Lord gave me more revelation about
the power of thanksgiving to open the gates to His presence.

I was soaring above a land, and below me I could see a heavy battle
being fought. I could hear the sounds of war—metal upon metal, as
weapons crashed against each other. The Lord was allowing me to see
the spiritual battle the Body of Christ was going through.

As I looked below me, searching to see with more clarity who exactly was in the battle and how it was that they were fighting, I saw a shift happen.

The many people who were in the battle fighting against demonic assaults, suddenly shifted their position. I saw that previously they had been fighting from a position of defense, from the ground looking up. But suddenly they moved to the offensive side. As I saw them rise up from the ground and sit above on the backs of mighty horses, I noticed their armor had changed as well—now it was much stronger and it covered them more. Now they were dressed in armor, ready to battle the enemy.

Then I saw the banners they carried. The words "Praise" and "Thanksgiving" were etched on the beautiful banners help up with their mighty arms. As I saw those banners swaying back and forth, a new sound was released in the mighty battle. Beautiful sounds of Heaven were released, with multitudes of voices singing; and at that, the enemy began to retreat and screech.

I watched as the mighty warriors marched on carrying the banners, swaying them back and forth. They were gaining ground. The demonic assaults lessened, and were easier to overthrow.

The more they marched on using the Banners of Praise and Thanksgiving, the thicker God's presence poured out, and the more the enemy had to back off.

So today, let us be not only be careful with our words, not complaining, but releasing words that bring our King Jesus glory. Let us be intentional. Set aside time to just simply praise and thank God, with no other agenda. Praise and thanksgiving are two of the most powerful weapons we have. But sometimes, if you're like me, you have to be intentional.

Let's raise high the banners today!

93

Carry Your Crown

THERE ARE TWO THINGS I AM CONVINCED ARE THE ENEMY'S GREAT-est desire to steal and rob from us: 1) our pure adoration and focus on Jesus alone, and 2) our confidence in Christ.

Knowing that as a child of God I am an heir, changes my perspective and strategy against the weapons that the enemy tries to attack me with. Confidence isn't a bad thing, but self-idolatry is a heavy fall. We can look at the devil's example as a big red flag thrown up to our own flesh. But wearing the mark of insignificance is not Jesus' desire, and is actually counter to what Scripture says.

> *Thus we have been set free to experience our rightful heritage. You can tell for sure that you are now fully adopted as his own children because God sent the Spirit of his Son into our lives crying out, "Papa! Father!" Doesn't that privilege of intimate conversation with God make it plain that you are not a slave, but a child? And if you are a child, you're also an heir, with complete access to the inheritance* (Galatians 4:5-7 The Message).

The Father met me in Heaven one day, in one of the most beautiful intimate ways. It was on Valentine's Day many years ago that the

Lord had asked me to write vows for Him. I was overseas as a missionary in Panama, and completely new to seeing in the supernatural, Heaven encounters, and Holy Spirit. And there He met me in the jungle.

That Valentine's Day, I came prepared with my wedding vows to Jesus, written by hand. I set aside time to just pray and wait on Him. "Now what, God," I asked out loud.

Suddenly I found myself in a vision right before the King of kings. I was in a beautiful room with a glass floor. Many people were present watching, but my eyes could only really focus on one person. Jesus was looking at me with a big smile across His face. This was one of my very first encounters seeing Jesus.

Sweeping me up in His arms, we danced around the great hall. As others watched, my continuous stare was at Him. As we danced, I felt His heart for me. I felt how much God truly loves me, in all my weakness, in all my impurities, He loves me.

Stopping the dance, Jesus looked right in my face and said, "You are not insignificant! You have to believe in yourself the way I do! You have to carry your crown." With that, the King placed a beautiful crown on my head. Its weight was new to balance.

The phrase "Christ within you, the hope of all glory," repeatedly was spoken by a voice somewhere in the room that I know now to be Holy Spirit's. Then as the vision was coming to a close, I heard the phrase again spoken by Jesus' loving voice, "Carry your crown. You are an heir."

Today, allow the Lord to remind you of your significance to Him. For you, Jesus went to the cross. God sacrificed His Son so that He may have relationship with *you*. Out of love He beckons you to continually look toward Him and pursue Him. You are an heir of Christ, and He stops at the sound of your prayers and voice. *He sees you.* You are known to Him. You matter.

94

Clarity of Focus

FIRE FELL AROUND ME, AS FAR AS MY EYES COULD SEE. THE CRACKING sound of trees falling was so loud it caused me to shudder. The wind was strong against my face and made a loud whizzing sound; it was hard to keep my eyes open. Debris was falling everywhere, and I felt like I was in danger.

"Where am I, God," I asked the Lord. "What are You showing me?"

Just then, I heard His voice loudly boom, "Clarity of focus, Ana, will carry you in this season." Then He provoked me with questions. With each daunting question, a tree would fall, causing the weight of the question to strike my core.

"Where are you going right now? What is the assignment I gave you for this season?" He asked. "Refocus and find your direction."

I pondered the questions. Right away I realized how my focus had been divided by other things pressing on me, instead of focusing on what God had originally asked me to do in this season.

"Who are you listening to right now? What's your biggest enemy?" Another large tree tumbled to the ground, and caused the earth to shake beneath my feet.

As I felt that tree come falling down, I instantly heard Holy Spirit whisper the answer. "Procrastination, discouragement, believing the lie of unimportance," I said out loud. As I heard myself say it, I was shocked a little. Here I had believed what was holding me back was all the enemy's doing. Granted he put those thoughts of discouragement and unimportance in my mind, but truth be told, I had agreed with him and now procrastination had set in. My agreement with him was my biggest enemy.

The heaviness and realization of the Lord's question weighed on me, "Who are you listening to right now?"

Boom! Another tree fell.

"What does the promised land look like? What have I promised you?" A pause and then, "Declare it and declare it again."

Clarity of focus will carry us through the hardest seasons of firing. After this vision, I spent some time just declaring "Clarity of focus," and as I did, my lens became clearer. I could see what was in the way. I could see what was distracting me from fulfilling my assignment from the Lord for that season. I could see God and hear Him with more clarity than ever.

Clarity of focus will not only carry you through the season, but will help you push through and get to the other side where you are walking in His promises. You have to see where you are going to get there. As a runner sees the goal, he can push through pain to get to the finish line. But he can't be distracted. A clear focus is the motivation to push through—believe you can and you will get there. A clear focus on Him and what God is saying will carry you.

> *Folly brings joy to the one who has no sense, but whoever has understanding keeps a straight course* (Proverbs 15:21 NIV).

95

Parcels Waiting

IN THIS PARTICULAR ROOM IN HEAVEN, ANGELS WERE BUSTLING about the room carrying parcels in their arms. As far as my eyes could see were large shelves lining the walls of the room. Searching through the shelves for the right packages, the angels would gather them in their arms and then turn and wait for a signal from Jesus. They were waiting for Jesus' instruction. Nodding His head toward them, they would drop down on the earth below to make their delivery.

"What are they doing?" I asked the Lord.

"Well, they are taking answers to the prayers of My saints down below. Each one is specifically assigned for the delivery of these special packages," He said.

Some angels were just standing and seemed to be waiting. They stood by the shelves, ready.

"Why are those angels not delivering the packages?" I asked the Lord.

"They are waiting," He smiled back at me.

I looked puzzled back at Him.

"They are waiting for My saints down below to pray and ask for what it is they need. For you see, these are the answer to their prayers, yet some do not ask. Ask, and it will be given to you; knock, and it will be opened. Some of these packages are timely too. The angels are waiting for my permission to make their delivery. My timing is always good and always perfect, for I am the Author and Creator of the universe. But Ana, you must always ask. Never give up partnering with Me and asking!"

Thousands of parcels lined the shelves, waiting.

Matthew 7:7 says, *"Ask, and it will be given to you; seek, and you will find; knock, and it will be opened to you."* So what can you ask God for today? Whether minuscular or enormous, He cares. So, what's on your heart? Perhaps the answer is just waiting for you to ask the question.

96

Currency of Heaven

I KNOW AND AM SURE THERE IS A CURRENCY OF HEAVEN THAT EXISTS. One day, my husband and I tapped into it.

We had just returned from living overseas as missionaries. With barely a few dollars to our name, and staying with my parents, I actually had peace about our finances. Or so I thought. That peace was challenged though.

My husband came to me one evening and said, "Guess what happened to me today?"

"What?" I asked.

"I was walking along this morning and I felt like I was supposed to look down. I did, and right there in front of me was a ten-dollar bill. So I picked it up."

"Ah, that's awesome," I said. My mind instantly started calculating how we could stretch that ten dollars really thin to purchase the most amount of groceries possible.

My husband continued, "But then later on, I saw a woman outside in a parking lot who needed money to buy food, so I gave the ten dollars to her."

"Wow," I said, as I selfishly thought about how we too needed food.

The next morning, my husband got up early, as he always does, to have prayer time and Bible study with the Lord. As he opened his Bible that morning to read, he saw a crisp, brand-new, one-hundred-dollar bill inside.

To this day, we never have found the person who gave us that money. We asked everyone we knew, and all denied it. God supplied.

Later that day, I was thanking the Lord for giving us that blessing that morning, and I heard His voice say, "Do not fret, My beloved. I will take care of your daily needs. Trust Me."

Just as Jesus miraculously fed the crowds of people with only five loaves and two fish, He replenishes us daily with what we need (Matt. 14:15-21). As you give—whatever that may be, not just money—the Lord blesses it and replenishes it. It's the currency of Heaven.

Look at the birds of the air, that they do not sow, nor reap nor gather into barns, and yet your heavenly Father feeds them. Are you not worth much more than they? Do not worry then.... But seek first His kingdom and His righteousness, and all these things will be added to you (Matthew 6:26,31,33).

97

Goodness and Pleasure of the Lord

THE LORD OFTEN REMINDS ME OF THE FOLLOWING ENCOUNTER when I need it.

I was sitting reading my Bible when I heard the voice of Jesus say, "I have something for you today." Shutting my Bible, I closed my eyes and just waited.

A radiant angel then approached me. She was adorned in a blueish-green gown, and light beamed off of her. I was taken aback by her beauty, and I could feel the presence of the Lord radiating in the room as she came near.

"Who are you?" I asked.

Smiling, she answered, "I have come to take you somewhere. Today, you are to feel His goodness and pleasure over you."

Next, I was led to a giant oak door. Upon opening it, I was blinded by the brightest light. Stumbling, I blindly walked toward the light. I could feel warmth and joy all over me.

Then I heard God's voice boom, "You are more comfortable with My power and presence than you are with My pleasure for you. This is another aspect of My presence you need to understand. From here you'll draw your strength. You need sit daily here with me and let me fill you with My goodness, love, and joy for you."

There is nothing like the love of the Father. It replaces everything, and at the same time washes everything away. Do you know today that He is pleased with you? He is proud of you.

All too often it's easier to embrace a picture of a correcting Father when we think of God. When facing a loving and good God, we realize our lack and incapability. Embracing our weakness requires us to embrace the reality of how undeserving we are. And yet He still loves us.

Today, are you comfortable with His love? Can you sit with it, and allow His goodness to wash over you? The power of God is wonderful, but the love of the Father, His goodness and pleasure, will sustain you.

Absolutely nothing can get between us and God's love because of the way that Jesus our Master has embraced us (Romans 8:39 The Message).

98

The Abiding Tree

I AM CONVINCED THAT GOD WILL REACH DOWN AND PURSUE US IN A place of encounter, whether we are pursuing Him or not. Granted it helps to pursue Him to step into an encounter, but out of desire for relationship, He pursues us sometimes when we're not even looking. I have heard person after person's testimonies of times when God broke into their world and took them by surprise.

He has always been after relationship with His children. He's been after our hearts before the beginning of time. He comes and crashes into our world, our everyday happenings, to reveal Himself.

When I first started seeing in the supernatural with God and experiencing Heaven encounters, I had certain expectations. "God take me today to Heaven. Show me something new," I would ask of Him.

And then He would show me something simple, or so I thought it was; when in reality it carried more depth.

A place of encounter—the Abiding Tree.

I would close my eyes, and instantly see myself before a golden tree. It was beautiful, gold with large flower blossoms and fruit. Jesus would be there, waiting for me to come join Him. Together we sat under the tree and talked heart to heart, holding nothing back from each other.

Smiling, He often would reach up and pick fruit for me to taste and enjoy. "Taste and see that I am good," He would say as He smiled and handed me the fruit. "It's that easy, Ana."

Now, although He's taken me many other places, and shown me many more things, this place, under this tree with the One I love the most, is my special place of encounter.

Many times I've come to the abiding tree with my heart in disarray. I carry burdens on my shoulders into my time of encounter with Jesus. He looks at me, smiles, and says the same thing, "Taste and see that I am good." And once again, hands me fruit, "It's that easy."

Sometimes religion overcomplicates the simplicity of the Gospel. *"Because He loved us first"* (1 John 4:19 New Living Translation), He pursues us. He pours out His love for us and we get to receive it. Not for what we do, but just because *He is love.* That's grace. The Father's love is the answer to a hurting world, and an encounter with it is the greatest experience we could ever desire. Just when I think I understand it, He takes me a little bit deeper, and a little bit farther into His heart, and I am undone.

Today, may you find your place of deep encounter with Jesus. He's waiting for you.

99

What's Impossible?

"…Make this valley full of trenches." For thus says the Lord, "You shall not see wind nor shall you see rain; yet that valley shall be filled with water, so that you shall drink, both you and your cattle and your beasts. This is but a slight thing in the sight of the Lord…" It happened in the morning about the time of offering the sacrifice, that behold, water came by the way of Edom, and the country was filled with water (2 Kings 3:16-18,20).

THE LORD'S VOICE SPOKE TO ME ONE DAY, CLEAR AS A BELL, "I AM THE God of the impossible!" It sounded like thunder, the strength of it was so loud. As this phrase came booming in, I felt fear being shaken off me. I had been struggling with a lot of fear of the unknown, looking at my circumstance with disbelief of what God had shown me He would do.

Have you ever been in a desert situation like the one this Scripture describes? In the natural, you look at your circumstance and wonder,

How God? How are You going to turn this around? Your hope is dried up, and expectancy is gone.

Or maybe you have reduced your dreams to something more practical and realistic; dreams that are within reach.

Following "I am the God of the impossible!" I heard the next phrase, "Believe in Me for the impossible! What's impossible for you? Ask Me for it."

So I sat back and wrestled with coming up with something completely impossible for me. Then an old dream started to stir within me again. With Holy Spirit's nudge, I placed it before the Lord and asked Him to breathe life into my old dream that had gathered dust on it. I prayed for a miracle that only He could do.

Just like that, an angel appeared before me. It winked at me! Can you believe that? It literally winked at me. Then it said, "Nothing's too hard. It's already in the works," and was gone.

Although you can't see it in the natural, can you muster up the faith to believe that today, "It's already in the works"? Disappointment often holds us back from daring to believe and dream again. Don't let disappointment restrain you from faith-filled prayers. Dare to believe that *He can and will do the impossible.*

So, what big dream do you have? If you don't have one yet, it's time to start dreaming with God! He can make the desert places an oasis of promises. Nothing is too hard or too out of reach for the King!

100

Choose Faith,
Not Fear

"ANA, IT'S NOW THAT YOU HAVE TO CHOOSE—FEAR OR FAITH? WHICH one will you build your life on?" Jesus asked me.

One of the most powerful and memorable encounters of my life happened at just the Lord's perfect and good timing. I was in a life-threatening situation that had hit our family—and I had to choose—faith or fear.

The Lord had taken me in a vision to a ledge of the Grand Canyon. There, a giant eagle soared beneath the ledge back and forth, back and forth, waiting for me to jump off and onto his back. My fear of heights was kicking up in full gear.

"But, God! It's so far! Couldn't we start this faith thing with like a five-foot drop instead of the Grand Canyon?" I cried out loud.

Long story short, I eventually did jump off that cliff. When I did, I fell, and I fell far! Terror pulsed through my body, as all I could see was the whirling ground below. Then suddenly, I landed on something really hard. "Ouch!" His timing is perfect.

I had landed on the back of the giant eagle. As we soared quickly through the air, wind whizzing through my hair, I heard the eagle say something to my surprise as it looked back at me.

"I told you I would be with you!" Then I realized I was riding on Holy Spirit!

I am convinced that fear is one of the most crippling tactics of the enemy. We allow fear to whisper into our ears, and our heart agrees with it quickly, even without our realization sometimes. Fear steps in and faith steps out. And then he has us—the robber, the enemy. We become victims of his assaults as we take our eyes off the Author of faith and fixate on our situation.

God makes all things new. Have faith.

He believes in you, when you don't. Have faith.

He is the God of miracles. Choose faith.

Faith is one of your best weapons.

> *Faith shows the reality of what we hope for; it is the evidence of things we cannot see* (Hebrews 11:1 New Living Translation).

Conclusive Prayer

Holy Spirit, thank You for being my Best Friend. You whisper and point to the mysteries of God. Hallelujah! God, You are bringing me to a deeper place of walking with You in daily encounters. I choose and pursue intimacy with You, Jesus, before everything else—and my great reward is knowing You more. Your love and blood shed for me covers every sin. I claim today my full inheritance—freedom, Heaven, healing, prosperity, joy, and to live life abundantly. Come now, and tear back the veil so that my spiritual eyes may be opened to see You. For Your Glory, God! Amen.

About the Author

Ana Werner and her husband, Sam, are the associate directors of the Heartland Healing Rooms in Lees Summit, Missouri. Ana travels internationally and equips people to see in the Spirit, move in the prophetic, and experience healing and deliverance through her ministry. Her transparency as she shares the realities and experiences she has had in Heaven brings the Holy Spirit, the love of the Father, and the power of God into the room when she speaks. Ana is passionate about leading people into encountering Jesus' heart.

For more information visit: anawerner.org